OPTIONS TRADING CRASH COURSE

The Beginner's Guide to Investing with Options Trading.
Know All You Need About Investing Strategies to
Generate Cash Flow.

by

Clark DAVISON

Disclaimer Notice

Please note the information contained within this document is for educational and entertainment purposes only. All effort has been executed to present accurate, up-to-date, and reliable, complete information. No warranties of any kind are declared or implied. Readers acknowledge that the author is not engaging in the rendering of legal, financial, medical, or professional advice. The content within this book has been derived from various sources. Please consult a licensed professional before attempting any techniques outlined in this book.

By reading this document, the reader agrees that under no circumstances is the author responsible for any losses, direct or indirect, which are incurred as a result of the use of the information contained within this document, including, but not limited to, — errors, omissions, or inaccuracies.

Table of Contents

INTRODUCTION

For savvy investors, options trading is a way to maximize assets and manage some of the risks associated with market play. Almost every investor is familiar with the saying, "buy low and sell high." But with options, if stocks are going up, down, or sideways, it is possible to benefit. With relatively small cash, you can use options to cut losses, preserve profits, and monitor large chunks of stock.

Option techniques, on the other hand, can be difficult and dangerous. Not only can you lose your entire investment, but you could also be exposed to potentially infinite losses by specific strategies.

So, it is significant to think about the impact of implied volatility and time decay on your strategy before you trade options. This book is going to help you answer those challenging questions. There is no need to think; turn to the approach.

The Option pricing model will not be derived here. It is one of those times we even discuss the model. That kind of thing is right to know, but the purpose here is to have the necessary information required to trade a particular strategy, not bore the pants off you entirely.

You can also find "Options Guy's Tips" in this book, which illustrates basic concepts or give you extra guidance on how to run a specific strategy. There's a big item next to them as an example of the value of these tips. To get the best of all information from this book, be sure to pay special attention.

I hope that you enjoy reading The Book of Option.

CHAPTER ONE

WHAT IS AN OPTION?

Options are financial instruments dependent on the valuation of underlying securities such as stocks, which are derivatives. An option contract gives the buyer the ability to purchase or sell the underlying asset, depending on the agreement they possess. Unlike futures, if they choose not to, the buyer is not forced to buy or sell the asset.

- Call options help the holder to purchase the asset within a particular timeframe at a specified price.
- Put options enable the holder to sell the asset within a specific timeframe at a stated price.

Each option agreement will have a fixed expiry date by which the holder is expected to exercise his or her option. The specified price is regarded as the strike price for an option. Options are usually acquired and sold by brokers that are online or retail.

Understanding Options

A flexible financial commodity is Options. These deals have a buyer and a seller, where the first pays a premium for the rights given by the contract for options. There is a bullish buyer and a bearish seller for each call option, while a bearish buyer and a bullish seller have put options.

Option contracts normally represent 100 shares of the underlying security, and for each contract, the buyer may pay a premium charge. For instance, if an option has a premium of 35 cents per contract, it will cost $35 ($0.35 x 100 = $35) to purchase one option. The premium is partly dependent on the strike price, until the expiry date, the price for buying or selling the safe. The expiration date is another factor in the premium amount. The expiry date specifies the day the option contract must be used, just as with the milk carton in the refrigerator. The underlying asset will determine a use-by date. For inventories, it is usually the third Friday of the month of the agreement.

For various reasons, traders and investors will purchase and sell options. Speculation of options enables an investor to hold a leveraged stake in an asset at a lower cost than purchasing its shares. Investors can use options to hedge or lower their portfolio's risk exposure. In certain situations, when they buy call options or become an option writer, the option holder will produce income. One of the most direct methods to invest in oil is also through options. The regular trading volume of the investment and open interest for options traders are the two main numbers to watch to make the most well-informed investment decisions.

American options may be applied at any time before the expiry date of the contract. In contrast, European options may be exercised either on the date of expiry or the exercise date. Exercising involves using the right to purchase the underlying security or sell it.

Option Risk Metrics: The Greeks

'Greeks' is a term regarding the options market to describe the various aspects of the risk involved in the positioning of an option, in a single option, or a portfolio of options. Since they are usually identified with Greek symbols, these variables are called Greeks. Each risk variable is a consequence of the option's flawed assumption or interaction with another underlying variable. To determine option risk and control option portfolios, traders use various Greek values, such as delta, Theta, etc.

THE DELTA

Delta (Δ) reflects the rate of change between the option's price and a \$1 change in the underlying asset price. In other words, the option's price sensitivity is proportional to the underlying option. A call option's delta has a range between zero and one, while a put option's delta has a range between zero and negative. Assume, for instance, that an investor has a long call option with a delta of 0.50. Thus if the underlying stock rises by $1, the option's price will potentially increase by 50 cents.

Delta also reflects the hedge ratio for options traders to establish a delta-neutral position. For example, you would need to sell 40 shares of stock to be entirely hedged if you buy a regular American call option with a 0.40 delta. A net delta for a portfolio of options can also be used to obtain the portfolio's hedge ratio.

The current probability that it will expire in-the-money is a less common use of an option's delta. For example, today, a 0.40 delta call option has an implied 40 percent likelihood of finishing in-the-money.

THE THETA

Theta (Θ) describes the rate of change between the option's price and time, or time sensitivity - also known as the time decay of the investment. Theta represents the sum that will decrease the cost of an option as the time to expiration decreases; everything things equal. For example, suppose an investor is long with a theta choice of -0.50. The option's price will decline by 50 cents per day that passes, everything else being equal. If three trading days pass, the value of the option will decrease by $1.50 potentially.

When options are at-the-money, Theta increases and decreases when options are in-and out-of-the-money, options near to expiry often have time decay-accelerating. Long calls and long puts will typically have negative Theta; positive Theta will be given to short calls and short puts. An instrument whose value is not diminished by time, such as a stock, will have zero Theta, by contrast.

THE GAMMA

Gamma (Γ) reflects the rate of difference between the delta of an option and the price of the underlying asset. It is called the price sensitivity of the second-order (second-derivative). Given a $1 step in the underlying defense, Gamma indicates the amount the delta will change. For instance, assume that an investor has a long one call option on hypothetical XYZ stock. The choice for calling has a delta of 0.50 and a gamma of 0.10. If stock XYZ, therefore, increases or decreases by $1, the delta of the call option will increase or decrease by 0.10.

Gamma is used to assess how stable the delta of an option is: higher gamma values suggest the delta will shift significantly in reaction to even minor fluctuations in the underlying price. Gamma is advanced for options that are at-the-money and lower for in and out-of-the-money options, and as expiration approaches accelerate in magnitude. Generally, the farther away from the expiration date, gamma values are smaller; choices with longer expirations are less vulnerable to delta shifts. Gamma values are usually larger as expiration progresses, as market fluctuations have a more significant effect on Gamma.

To be delta-gamma neutral, options traders can opt not only for hedge delta but also for Gamma, meaning that the delta will remain close to zero as the underlying price moves.

VEGA

Vega (V) illustrates the rate of change between an option's value and the underlying asset's implied volatility. It is the option's volatility sensitivity. Vega displays the sum of price increases of an option given a 1 percent rise in implied volatility. For example, a Vega option of 0.10 means that if the implied volatility increases by 1 percent, the option's value is expected to change by 10 cents.

Since increased volatility means that extreme values are more likely to be encountered by the underlying instrument, an increase in volatility would increase an option's value accordingly. Conversely, the value of the option would be negatively affected by a decline in volatility. For at-the-money options that have more extended periods before expiration, Vega is at its limit.

It can be pointed out by those familiar with the Greek language that there is no actual Greek letter called Vega. Different hypotheses of how this symbol made its way into stock-trading lingo, resembling the Greek letter nu.

THE RHO

Rho (p) reflects the rate of change between an option's value and an interest rate change of 1 percent. It tests the interest rate response. For instance, assume that a call option has a 0.05 rho and a $1.25 price. If interest rates increase by 1%, the call option's value will rise to $1.30, everything else being equal. In this case of put options, the opposite is valid. Rho is highest with long periods before expiration for at-the-money options.

GREEKS MINOR

Lambda, Epsilon, Vomma, Vera, Pace, Zomma, Color, Ultima are some other Greeks who are not mentioned as much.

These Greeks are second or third derivatives of the pricing model and affect factors such as the delta shift with volatility shifts. In options trading strategies, they are increasingly used as computer software can rapidly compute and account for these dynamic and often esoteric risk factors.

Profits and Risks from Buying Call Options

As stated earlier, the call options allow the holder to purchase at the stated strike price underlying security by the expiry date called the expiry. If they do not wish to buy the asset, they have no responsibility to purchase the asset. The threat to the buyer of the call option is limited to the premium charged. There is no effect on the volatility of the underlying stock.

Buyers of call options are bullish on a stock and hope the share price would rise above the strike price before the contract expiry. If the investor's bullish viewpoint is realized and the stock price rises above the strike price, the investor may exercise the option of purchasing the stock at the strike price and selling the stock immediately for a profit at the current market price.

Their benefit on this trade is the price of market share less the price of strike share plus the cost of the option-the premium and any commission for a brokerage to position the orders. The result will be multiplied by the number of purchased option contracts, multiplied by 100, assuming 100 shares are represented in each agreement.

However, if the underlying stock price doesn't move above the strike price by the expiry date, the option expires in vain. The holder is not forced to purchase the shares, but the call's premium will be lost.

Profits and Risks from Selling Call Options

Selling choices for calling is known as writing a contract. The artist pays the premium fee. In other terms, the premium would be paid by an option buyer to the writer or seller of an option. When selling the option, the maximum benefit is the premium paid. An investor that sells a call option is bearish and expects that the price of the underlying stock will decrease or stay reasonably close to the option's strike price over the life of the option.

Whether the prevailing market share price is at or below the strike price by expiry, the option expires in vain for the call buyer. The seller of the option pockets the premium as their benefit. The option is not exercised because, at the strike price above or equal to the prevailing market price, the option holder will not purchase the stock.

However, if the market share price reaches the strike price at the expiry date, the option's seller must sell the shares at the lower strike price to the option's buyer. In other terms, to sell to the call option purchaser, the seller must either sell shares from their portfolio holdings or buy the stock at the prevailing market price. The writer of the contract incurs a loss. How significant a loss depends on the cost basis of the shares they need to use to finance the option order, plus the brokerage order's costs, but minus any premium they got.

The danger to the call authors, as you can see, is much greater than the risk exposure of call purchasers. The buyer of the call just loses the premium. Since the stock price will continue to increase losses dramatically, the writer faces infinite risk.

Profits and Risks from Buying Put Options

Put options are transactions where the buyer expects the market price of the underlying stock will fall below the strike price on or before the option's expiration date. Again, without the requirement to sell at the stated strike per-share price by the indicated date, the holder may sell shares.

Since owners of put options want to reduce the stock price, when the underlying stock's price is below the strike price, the put option is profitable. If the prevailing market price is lower than the expiry strike price, the investor can exercise the right to exercise that right. They are going to sell shares at the higher strike price of the contract. They can purchase them on the open market if they wish to substitute their holding of these shares.

Their profit on the trade is the strike price plus costs, the premium, and any brokerage fee to position the orders, less the current market price. The result will be multiplied by the number of purchased option contracts, multiplied by 100, assuming 100 shares are represented in each agreement.

If the underlying stock price reduces, the value of owning a put option will increase. Conversely, as the stock price rises, the value of the put option decreases. If the option expires worthlessly, the risk of purchasing put options is limited to losing the premium.

Profits and Risks from Selling Put Options

Often known as drafting a contract is selling put options. A writer of a put option expects that the underlying stock price will remain the same or rise over the option's life, making them bullish on the shares. The option buyer has the right to making the seller buy shares of the underlying asset at the expiring strike price.

If the underlying stock's value closes above the strike price by the expiry date, the put option expires worthlessly. The net benefit of the writer is the premium. The option is not used because the option holder will not sell the stock when the market price is higher at the lower strike share price.

However, if the stock's market cost falls below the contract's strike price, the put option writer is forced to purchase the underlying stock's shares at the strike price. In other terms, the put option will be exercised by the buyer of the option. As it is greater than the stock market value, the seller can sell their shares at the strike price.

If the market's price falls below the strike price, the put option writer's risk arises. Now at expiration, at the strike price, the seller is required to buy shares. The loss of the put writer may be significant, depending on how much the stocks have appreciated.

The put editor, the seller, may either hang on to the stocks and expect the stock price to rise above the purchase price, sell the stocks and take the loss. Any loss, however, is compensated somewhat by the earned premium.

An investor would often write put options at a strike price that is where they see a good offer for the stocks and will be willing to buy at that price. When the price falls, they get the stock at the price they want with the bonus of earning the option premium, and the option holder exercises their option.

The Pros

- When the stock price is rising, a call option holder can purchase assets at a lower price than the market.

- If the market price is below the strike price, the put option purchaser will benefit from selling the stock at the strike price.
- Sellers of options receive a premium fee for writing an option from the buyer.

The Cons

- The put option seller will be forced to purchase the asset at a higher strike price in a declining market than they would usually pay on the market.
- If the stock's price increases dramatically, and they are forced to buy shares at a high price, the call option writer faces infinite risk.
- Purchasers of options must pay the writers of the contract an upfront premium.

Real-World Example of An Option

Suppose that shares in Microsoft (MFST) trade at $108 per share, and you think they're going to rise in value. To profit from a growth in the stock's price, you decide to purchase a call option.

For 37 cents per touch, you buy one call option with a strike price of $115 for one month in the future. Your gross cash outlay is $37, plus fees and commissions (0.37 x 100 = $37) for the job.

Your option will be worth one if the stock increases to $116 because you will exercise the option to buy the stock for $115 per share and resell it immediately for $116 per share. Since you paid 37 cents and received $1, the profit on the option stake will be 170.3 percent, which is much more than the 7.4 percent rise in the underlying stock price from $108 to $116 at the time of expiry.

In other words, when one option contract represents 100 shares ($1 - 0.37 x 100 = $63), the benefit in dollar terms will be a net of 63 cents, or $63.

Your option would expire worthlessly if the stock dropped to $100, and you would be out with a $37 premium. The upside is that at $108, you did not buy 100 shares, which would have resulted in a net loss of $8 per share, or $800. Options will help minimize your downside risk, as you can see.

Options Spreads

Options spreads are strategies used in various combinations for a desired risk-return profile to purchase and sell different options. Spreads are designed using vanilla options and can take advantage of different situations, such as conditions of high or low volatility, up or down movements, or everything in between.

Spread strategies, such as bull call spreads or iron condors, may be characterized by their payoff or profit-loss profile visualizations. See our article on ten popular techniques for spreading options to learn more about items like covered calls, straddles, and calendar spreads.

Types of Options

There are several different kinds of options that can be traded, and in a variety of ways, these can be classified. Two key forms exist in a vast sense: calls and puts. Calls give the customer the right to purchase the underlying property, while places provide the customer the right to sell the underlying property. In addition to this simple differentiation, choices are often generally categorized based on whether they are American or European style. It has nothing to do with geographic position, but rather when necessary to exercise the contracts. More about the discrepancies can be read below.

Depending on how they are traded, their maturity cycle, and the underlying protection, options can be further classified. Other unique types exist and a range of exotic alternatives. We have published a detailed list of the most common categories on this website and the various forms that fall into these categories. We also provided further information on each type.

- Calls
- Puts
- American Design
- European Theme
- Exchanged Options for Swap
- Over Counter Options
- Form by Expiration choice
- Option Form by Protection Underlying Option
- Employee Stock Options
- Cash Settled Options
- Exotic options

CALLS

Call options give the owner the right, at a negotiated price, to purchase the underlying asset in the future. If you assumed that the underlying asset was likely to rise in price over a given period, you would buy a call. Calls have an expiry date, and the underlying asset may be obtained at any time before the expiry date or on the expiry date. This way is depending on the terms of the contract. For more comprehensive details and some examples of this kind, please visit the Calls page below.

PUTS

Put options are simply the reverse of calls. The owner of a position has the right to sell the underlying asset at a pre-determined price in the future. Therefore, if you were expecting the underlying asset to fall in value, you might purchase a put. As with calls, the touch has an expiration date. For more information and examples of how options work, please read the following page-Puts.

AMERICA STYLE

About options, the word "American style" has nothing to do with where contracts are obtained or sold, but rather with the conditions of the agreements. Options contracts come with an expiry date, at which stage the owner is entitled to purchase or sell the underlying security (if a call) (if a put). With American-style options, the contract owner also has the freedom to exercise the right at any point before the expiry date. An obvious benefit to the owner of an American type contract is this extra flexibility. More information, and working examples, can be found on the following page, American Style Choices.

EUROPE STYLE

The contracts for European style options are not provided with the same flexibility as American style contracts. You have the right to purchase or sell the underlying asset on which the contract is based only on the expiry date and not before if you hold a European type contract. For more information on this style, please read the following page - European Style Choices.

EXCHANGE TRADED OPTIONS

It is the most prevalent type of option, also known as listed options. Any options contract listed on a public trading exchange is defined by the word 'Exchanged Traded.' Using the services of an appropriate broker, they can be purchased and sold by anyone.

OVER THE COUNTER OPTIONS

'Over The Counter' (OTC) options are exchanged only in the OTC markets, making them less available to the general public. They appear to be more complex terms for personalized contracts than most exchanges traded contracts.

Option Type by Underlying Security

If individuals use the word options, they usually apply to stock options, where shares in a publicly-traded corporation are the underlying asset. While these are very prevalent, there are also various other forms where something else is the underlying defense. With a summary, we have described the most common of these below.

Stock Options: Shares in a particular publicly-traded company are the underlying collateral for these contracts.

Index Options: These are somewhat similar to stock options, except for an index such as the S&P 500 index instead of the underlying security being stocks in a particular business.

Forex/Currency Options: Contracts of this form give the purchaser the right at a negotiated exchange rate to buy or sell a specific currency.

Futures Options: A defined futures contract is the underlying protection for this type. In essence, a futures option gives the owner the right to enter into the given futures contract.

Commodity Options: A real commodity or a commodity futures contract may be the underlying asset for an agreement of this kind.

Basket options: This is based on the underlying benefit of a securities group that may consist of bonds, currencies, commodities, or other financial instruments.

Option Type by Expiration

Contracts can be defined by their expiry cycle, which refers to the point at which the owner has to exercise his right to purchase or sell the related asset under the terms of the contract. Some contracts are only available for one particular form of the expiry period, although you can choose some contracts. This data is far from necessary for most traders of options, but it helps understand the words. Here are some descriptions of the various forms of contracts based on their period of expiration.

Normal options: These are based on the standardized expiry intervals in which contracts for options are specified. You will have the option of at least four different expiration months to choose from when buying an agreement of this kind. The reasons that exist in the way they do for these expiration periods are due to limitations placed in place when options were first implemented when they should be traded. Expiration cycles can get very complicated, but what you need to remember is that from a list of at least four separate months, you will be able to pick your desired expiration date.

Weekly Options: Sometimes referred to as weekly options, launched in 2005. They are currently only available on a small range of underlying securities, including some of the major indices, but are growing in popularity. The basic weekly concept is the same as standard choices, but they only have a much shorter expiration duration.

Quarterly options: Also known as quarterly options, these are listed on exchanges with expiry dates for the next four quarters plus the final quarter of the following year. Quarterly contracts expire on the last day of the expiration month, unlike standard agreements that expire on the third Friday of the expiration month.

Long-term expiry anticipation securities: These long-term contracts are commonly referred to as LEAPS and are available on a reasonably wide variety of underlying securities. LEAPS still expire in January but can be purchased for the next three years with expiry dates.

Employee Stock Options

It's a type of stock option in which contracts based on the business's stock for which they work are given to employees. In general, they are used as a form of remuneration, bonus, or motivation to enter a company. On the following tab, Employee Stock Options, you can learn more about them.

Cash Settled Options

Cash-settled contracts, when exercised or settled, do not require the physical transfer of the underlying asset. Instead, the other party is paid in cash by whichever party to the deal has made a profit. These contracts are usually used when it is impossible or costly for the underlying asset to pass to the other party. On the following tab, Cash Settled Options, you will find more.

Exotic Options

The exotic choice is a concept used to refer to a contract with more complicated clauses that have been personalized. Non-Standardized options are also graded. A plethora of different exotic agreements exists, many of which are only available on the OTC markets. However, some exotic contracts are becoming more popular with mainstream investors and are listed on government exchanges. Some of the more common forms are given below.

Barrier Options: These contracts provide the holder with a pay-out if the underlying security hits a pre-determined price (or does not, depending on the terms of the agreement). Please read the following page for more information: Barrier Options.

Binary Options: When a contract of this sort ends for the owner's benefit, a fixed sum of money is awarded. For more information on these contracts, please visit the following page: Binary Options.

Choose Options: These options were called "Chooser" since they allow the contract owner to select whether it is a call or a put when a specific date is reached.

Compound Options: These are options in which another option contract is the underlying security.

Look Back Options: This type of contract does not have a strike price but instead enables the owner to exercise the contract period's underlying protection at the best price. For examples and additional info, please visit the Look Back Options page below.

Risks Management with Options

Most investors erroneously assume that options are always riskier investments than stocks because they do not entirely understand what options are and how they function. Options are used to hedge positions and reduce risk, such as defensive packages. Options may also be used to bet on a stock going up or down. But with comparatively less risk than the real equivalent of the underlying stock being held or shortened. This article's emphasis will be on this latter use of options to mitigate risk in making directional bets. Read on to learn how the future risk of options positions can be measured and how the power of leverage can operate in your favor.

Are there risk-taker options or risk-averse options?

Most of the emphasis here is on exploring the most fundamental choice and building principles from there.

The other main emphasis is on directing your knowledge of how options work. That awareness enables you to use choices efficiently.

It is easy for someone who considers himself an instructor in options to advise people that if they expect the underlying stock price to rally and buy puts when they wish a fall, they can purchase call options. That will be a significant disservice to those readers, however. Using options is so much more than guessing whether stocks are going to move higher or lower. By the way, it's much more challenging to benefit from the guesswork than it sounds.

As risk-reducing devices, options were invented. They have been created to transfer risk from those who want to escape too much risk. Also, to those who are willing (for a fee) to embrace the risk, be more precise. If it sounds like it is possible to use alternatives as insurance plans, that's because they are. Many entrants to the world of options never get exposed to the principle of risk mitigation and therefore end up using options like a gambler might do. As someone who needs less risk when trading in the stock market, we advise you to use options.

The final decision is yours on how you use alternatives. Our task is to make sure readers understand the difference between risk speculation and hedging—so they can make wise choices. Most articles, therefore, apply to ways of generating profit with less risk (i.e., with less money on the line).

Avoiding Risk vs. Speculating

When you purchase policies for homeowners, you make a bet with the insurance provider. The insurance provider promises to provide money to repair your home, if it is lost, for a too (high) charge (premium). You have no intention of winning the bet. You hope that the new insurance policy will expire. However, if the unexpected arises, you purchase insurance because you cannot repair your home. So, you buy insurance for the peace of mind it brings.

A risk-averse stockholder can do the same. The stockholder is promised (for the life of the contract) that the stock's value will not fall below a specific price level by paying a premium to purchase a put option (the strike price of the option). Time passes, the insurance policy gaps, or the put option expires, as often happens with homeowner insurance, and the cost of insuring the property is lost. For most individuals, the question is whether the expense was worth the peace of mind it offers.

When dealing with a home, the response is almost always 'yes.' Stockholders ought to make a cautious determination, as a costly form of insurance is to purchase puts.

The point is to make sure that you are conscious of this:

- Purchasers appear to come in two types—Conservative stock-owning investors. The bullish investor is prepared to gamble that the stock price is going to fall.

Sellers are almost always speculating (this is not the time to talk about exceptions) by betting that the stock price will not decrease, or at least that it will not decrease sufficiently to lead to a monetary loss.

[Do you like this book? If so, I would be really happy if you could leave a short review on amazon, Thank You.]

http://www.amazon.com/gp/product-review/B08X31SNMZ

CHAPTER TWO

OPTIONS TRADING BASICS REVIEW

Description of stock options: If you purchase or own a stock option contract, you have the right, but not the duty, to buy or sell stock at a fixed price on or before the date of the deal (period).

Your contract expires after this date, and your option ceases to exist. Another name used for stock options is derivatives.

Stock options are contracts; there is nothing in which they reflect ownership. They are merely agreements that grant specific privileges to you.

Trading options (the buying side) can be described as buying contracts that you think will increase in value, and you can sell them at a higher price and pocket the difference once they rise in value.

1 contract for a stock option = 100 shares of a company's stock. You are buying the right to purchase or sell 100 shares of that stock when you buy 1 contract.

Puts and Calls: Two ways to make money with stock options

The "**Put option**" gives buyers the right, but not the duty, to "sell the stock at a set price on or before the date specified".

The "**Call option**" offers the right, but not the duty, to "buy a stock at a set price on or before the date specified".

- When you believe the price of the underlying stock will go up, you buy a call option.
- When you think the price of the underlying stock will go down, you buy a put option.

Puts and Calls expire on the 3rd Friday of the expiration month for trading purposes. For example, if I purchased a December option, it would cease to exist after the 3rd Friday in December (expire worthlessly).

If you're looking for a less Dangerous, Reliable way to be, Try The "Buffett Strategy" Profitable with Options.

What brought you to my page, I don't know. You may be interested in options to help you lower the risk of your other stock market holdings.

Maybe you are looking for a way to produce a little extra retirement income. Or perhaps you've just learned about choices, you're not sure what they are, and you want a clear step-by-step guide to getting started with them and knowing them.

I have no idea whether options are even right for you, but I promise to show you what has worked for me and the precise measures I have taken to gain extra money, protect my savings, and enjoy my life's freedom.

Option Contract

What's an Option Contract?

An option contract is a contract that gives the option holder the right to purchase. Or also sell the underlying asset at a specified price (known as the expiry date or maturity date) at a specified price (known as the strike price or exercise price) at a specific date (called the expiry date or maturity date). In contrast, the option seller or writer has no choice but to deliver or purchase the underlying asset if the option is exercised.

All sorts of arrangements come with contracts to purchase and sell. One of the lesser-known forms of contracts is known as an "option contract." The seller chooses to hold an offer open for a specified amount of time in a standard option contract. In return, a prospective buyer has to give the seller some payment. In other terms, the seller decides to hold the "option available to the buyer in an option contract".

Options Contracts at a glance

Options contracts are most often related to the financial services industry, where a seller may opt for a fixed period to buy the stock at a specific price. The seller has bargained away the right to withdraw the bid by accepting a certain sum of money in return for this option. However, it is necessary to figure out that there is no requirement for the party purchasing the option to exercise this option and buy the stock because they only negotiated the investment.

These contracts are also standard in real estate, where, among other steps, it can take a while for a prospective buyer to perform a full property inspection and obtain financing. In this situation, for example, the seller and the prospective buyer can agree on a certain amount, but before making a full commitment, the buyer needs to meet with her bank. If the buyer agrees to the conditions within the defined period, then a binding contract for the deal is made.

The option terminates at the end of the term indicated in the contract, irrespective of whether the purchaser exercises the option.

The Usefulness of Options contracts

Option contracts may seem overly complicated at first glance. However, in markets where rates fluctuate rapidly, options contracts are advantageous. Consider this instance:

Suppose you are an investor in a clothing manufacturer and you want to purchase stock. You note that prices are low for clothing manufacturers, at $2.00 a share, but you still want to do some research into an exciting business. So in return for their agreement to sell you the stock at its current price at any point in the next three months, you pay the company a small sum of money, such as 2 cents per Share. A breach of contract is considered a failure to hold this option available.

Two weeks later, the business you're studying is featured in a famous fashion magazine, and the stock skyrockets to $50 per share while you're still busy researching the apparel industry. Fortunately, your option contract is still in effect, and for just $2 per share, you can even buy the stock. You've purchased a $50 stock for a total cost of $2.02 per share, thanks to your smart planning.

As part of a compensation package, some companies offer options contracts. It is particularly true of start-up firms. Employee option contracts also offer workers the option at a much-reduced price to purchase company stock. Both the corporation and the worker then hope that the company's stock would increase rapidly.

The contract is made up of 2 Parties.

1. **Option Holder or Buyer of the option:** to agree, it costs the initial fee. The buyer of the call option gains from price increases but has little downside risk in price reductions since the option premium is most likely to lose. Similarly, in the case of price increases, the put option purchaser gains from price reduction but has minimal downside risk. In short, they restrict the downside risk of the investor while leaving the opportunity for the upside limitless.

2. **Option Seller or Writer of the Option:** earns the premium to bear the risk upon initiation of the option contract. The call writer gains from a price reduction but has an infinite upside risk in price increases. Likewise, if price increases, put writer advantages as he can retain the premium but lose a significant price decrease.

Stock options, stock indexes, futures contracts, foreign currencies, and other securities are currently traded.

Types & Examples of a Contract Option

#1 Call Option

It gives the owner the right to purchase an underlying asset at the expiration date at a strike price. The call owner is bullish on the underlying assets' movement (expects the stock price to rise). Let's take an example. Consider an investor with a strike of $7820 who buys the call option. The market price is $7600, the expiry date is four months, and the option price to buy one share is $50.

Long Call Payment Per-Share = [MAX (Stock Price – Strike Price, 0) – Upfront Premium Per Share]

- **Case 1:** the option will be exercised if the stock price at expiry is $7920 and the buyer will purchase it @ $7820 and sell it immediately on the market for $7920, realizing a benefit of $100 considering $50 in the upfront premium charged, the net profit is $50.

- **Case 2:** the option holder can prefer not to exercise if the stock price at expiration is $7700 because there is no point in purchasing it at $7820 when the stock's market price is $7700. The net loss is $50, despite the $50 initial premium.

#2-Put Option

It provides the holder the right to sell the underlying asset's strike price at the expiration date. The put holder is bearish (expects the stock price to fall) on the stock price movement. Let's take an example. Consider an investor with a $7550 strike who buys the put option. The market price is $7600, the expiry date is in three months, and the cost of one share purchase option is $50.

Long Put Payment Per-Share = [MAX (Strike Price – Stock Price, 0) – Upfront best Per Share]

- **Case 1:** if the stock price at termination is $7300, the investor can buy the asset at $7300 on the market and sell it to realize $250.00 under the terms of the put option @7550. The net profit is $200, given the $50 upfront premium charged.
- **Case 2:** the put option expires worthless if the stock price at expiration is $7700, and the investor loses $50, which is the upfront premium.

Uses of Option Contracts

#1-The Speculation

The investor takes the place of preference. He assumes that the stock price is currently selling at a lower price but will increase dramatically in the future, contributing to the benefit.

He believes that a stock's market price is trading at a higher price but will drop to profit in the future. They are betting on a market variable's future course.

#2-The hedging

The investor already has an asset exposure but uses the option contract to avoid the possibility of an adverse market element movement.

Options Contracts Are Exchange-Traded or Over the Counter

In terms of expiration dates, contract duration, strike price, position limits, and exercise limits, Exchange-Traded Options have standardized features. They are traded on an exchange where there is minimum default risk.

Over the counter, to suit their requirements, solutions may be customized by private parties. Since the choice writer is privately negotiated, he will default on his obligation. The counter market post-1980 is much larger than the exchange-traded market.

The option may be either American or European: the American option may be exercised up to the expiry date at any time, while the European option may be exercised only on the expiry date itself. The bulk of the exchange options traded are

European options, which are easier to evaluate than American options.

Drivers of the Option Contract Value

1. Volatility of the underlying stock: Measures how indeterminate we are about future price fluctuations. The probability of the stock to appreciate or depreciate rises as uncertainty increases. The greater the volatility of the stock, the greater the value of the option.

2. Period to Maturity: The longer the time left to expire, the greater the option value. Compared to shorter maturity contracts, more extended maturity options are valuable.

3. The trajectory of the underlying stock: If the stock appreciates, the call option will have a positive effect, and the options placed on it will have a negative impact. It will have the opposite effect if the stock falls.

4. Risk-free rate: The expected return required by investors continues to rise as the interest rate rises. Moreover, when using a higher discount rate, discounting the potential stream of cash flows to present value results in a decrease in the option value. The combined impact increases the value of the option to call and reduces the value of the option to put.

The Merits of Option Contract

- **Provide insurance:** Investors may use option agreements to shield themselves from unfavorable price movements while also enabling them to benefit from favorable price movements.

- **Lower Capital Requirement:** Investors can take stock market exposure by paying an initial premium lower than the actual stock price.

- **Risk/reward ratio:** Some methods allow the investor to make substantial gains while the loss is restricted to the premium charged.

The Demerits of Option Contract

- **Time Decay:** The option contract time value of the options declines as maturity approaches.

- **Involves Initial Investment:** If the option is not exercised, the holder is expected to pay an upfront non-refundable fee that can be lost. The option premium associated with the contract can be very high during volatile markets.

- **Shape Leverage:** A double-edged sword is a choice deal. If the price does not shift as planned, it magnifies the financial implications resulting in huge losses.

CHAPTER THREE

UNDERLYING OPTION SECURITY

A portfolio, index, bond, currency, or commodity on which an option's value is based is underlying option security. It is the critical component of how the alternative gets its worth. It is the reason why derivatives are listed as options. They derive their value from an underlying security's efficiency or price action.

Knowing Underlying Option Securities

A call option on Apple stock, for example, gives the holder the right, but not the duty, to buy Apple stock at a price stated in the option agreement. In this instance, the underlying option of security is Apple stock.

Many commonly used derivatives, including options, exist, but they all have one thing in common. Their value is dependent on an underlying asset or underlying security. The pricing of the options based on it would inevitably influence price changes in the underlying security.

The underlying security is sometimes referred to only as of the underlying in options and all derivative terms. Any index, asset, financial instrument, or even another derivative may be underlying security. Traders use options to either bet on or hedge against the underlying option security's potential price fluctuations. Combining the options used will further adapt the approach's functionality to particular suit requirements, enabling highly personalized risk management.

The Influence of the Underlying Option Security

The role of the underlying defense is to be itself. If there were no options, the underlying traders would buy and sell. However, the underlying item is the item that must be presented in the options contract by one party and agreed upon by the other party. The exception is where the underlying index is an index where only cash is exchanged at the end of the options contract.

The underlying factor is also critical for the pricing of options. The relationship between the underlying and its alternatives is not linear, although some options can hedge some options to simulate a linear relationship. Many features define the degree of non-linearity in option pricing models. These are called the Greeks because different Greek letters represent them.

For example, the further the strike price for an out-of-the-money option is from the current price of the underlying option's security, the less the cost of the option changes per unit of movement in the underlying option. The investment has a low delta value in this case. For options that have plenty of time left before maturity, the same is true. Theta determines it. Time decay grows as expiration approaches.

Conversely, in-the-money options and very close to expiration will switch with the underlying security option almost in lockstep.

How do you decide on spreads for Credit or Debit Options?

Some choices, like the way you put your jeans on, are easy. Not only are you most likely to go with the one-leg-at-a-time form, fly-in-the-front, but it's also the apparent option. You need to know whether you think the stock would go up or down if you trade options, but you have to remember volatility (Vol), too. Is it low or high? From here, will it go up or down? It is where strategic traders get hung up. Once you have the data you need, which options do you run with to spread? Is there a way to simplify the process of decision making? Maybe.

In particular vertical spreads are guilty of confounding even the best of them. A vertical spread is a given risk strategy that allows you to make bullish or bearish speculative trades, you might remember. And they are versatile. With minimal risk or a lot of risks, you can build a vertical. Short-term speculation or long-term directional play may be a vertical one.

Too Many Ways to Trade them

Vertical spreads are easy. They consist of either a long and short call or the same expiration of a long and short call. Remember, if we speak about bullish verticals, long call verticals for debit or short put verticals for a loan are the two options. If we're talking about bearish verticals, your options for a debit or short call verticals for credit are long put verticals. Now consider the issue of 64,000 dollars: Which one should you choose? Spreading debits or spreading credits? In cash or out of cash (OTM)? Expiration, what about? Selecting a vertical can sense like a daunting challenge when you're faced with an assortment of call and put options, with maybe hundreds of strike prices and expirations.

Ok, not afraid. A simple checklist of easy metrics that lets you select with confidence is what you should think. There are no assurances, as in all trading practices. This checklist is away, not necessarily the endpoint, to get started. It would help if you also decided, as an options trader, whether a specific vertical is a right choice. But a successful checklist will help the decision-making process move quicker so that new future opportunities can be taken advantage of.

Phase 1: check IV Percentile

Start with Vol when trading options, more precisely, whether a stock or index options volume is relatively high or low. Let's be straight now. It can always go higher, no matter how high the volume might be. And it can still go lower, no matter how low it may be (unless it's zero). So put the current volume in perspective via the "IV percentile", for instance. It is a measure that compares the recent overall implied volatility (IV) of the options of an underlying to its previous highs and lows.

Know the Percentile of Current IV.

In this example, the stock shows an IV percentile at 22 percent. You can find the data used for the IV percentile calculation in Today's Options Statistics section. "There are the "52 week IV High" and "52 week IV Low" in addition to the IV number, which is the total IV for the symbol you are looking at. If the 52-week IV high is 50 percent, the 52-week IV low is 19 percent, and the IV is 25.8 percent, then the IV percentile is 22 percent.

How to Calculate: The IV percentile formula adopts the current IV, subtracts the low IV of 52 weeks, and then splits it by the high IV of 52 weeks minus the low IV of 52 weeks. That is (25.8% to 19%)/ (50 percent to 19%) = 22 percent. It's fairly easy, so you save time because it's measured for you.

The higher the percentile of the IV, the closer it gets to its high of 52 weeks. The lower the percentile of the IV, the closer it is to its low of 52 weeks. The new IV is in the center of its 52-week high and low IV values, a 50 percent IV percentile, and that's a benchmark to remember while using debit or credit strategies.

On the Charts page, you can also take a look at the Imp Volatility analysis. The historical values of the total IV number used in the IV percentile formula are shown in this report. When the 52-week low and high IV values have occurred, you can also estimate. The IV percentile can often be skewed by a short-term increase or fall in the underlying IV. It could help you recognize where that happened and give you a larger understanding of that IV percentile figure.

How can an intravenous percentile help? It makes credit spreads more costly when IV is higher. The short 47/48 put spread, for instance, with a stock at $50, could have a theoretical value of 0.25 when IV is 15 percent, but 0.35 when IV is 25 percent. If the stock is above $48 at termination and a maximum potential loss of $75 if the stock is below $47 at expiration, shortening the 47/48 put spread for a 0.25 credit will give you a maximum potential profit of $25. Shorting the 0.35 credit spread of 47/48 would give you a maximum possible benefit of $35 and a maximum potential loss of $65.

Selling the spread for a loan of 0.35 gives you a more significant potential benefit and a lower possible loss than selling it for a loan of 0.25. A higher percentile IV, say, when it's over 50%, might mean a situation where a stock's short verticals might give you greater credits.

Similarly, when IV is lower when IV is higher, it will make the loan spreads less costly and offer smaller potential profits and greater potential losses relative to verticals at the same strike price. When the percentile IV is less than 50 percent, you might instead suggest debit spreads.

So if the IV percentile is, say, above 50%, you might pick trades by looking at credit spreads-short spreads if you're bullish; if you're bearish, short call spreads. If the IV percentile is less than 50 percent, you can pick trades by looking at debit spreads-long call spreads if you're bullish; if you're bearish, long put spreads.

You may want to choose verticals by choosing an expiration that fits the time frame for your directional trade after looking at the IV percentile when it is above 50 percent. Let's say you want to speculate that in the next 60 days, a stock could grow.

Find an expiration near 60 days in this scenario, then open up the option chain.

Phase 2: Assess the placement of strikes

How do you find an alternative that is part of that short put vertical to consider selling?

How to put a Vertical Spread

Go to the Trading tab and pull up an Option Chain to trade vertical spreads on the Thinkorswim platform from TD Ameritrade.

1. Choose either the bid or the asking price of one of the vertical options.

2. To create a short debit spread or long credit spread, then select Buy or Sell. A proposed range may be loaded into the Order Entry Tools when you do that. By default, using the strikes adjacent to the strike you have selected, the vertical will be created. If you choose a call, the next higher strike price will be used to create the vertical. The put utilized to generate the upright will be at the next lower strike price if you select a put.

- You can select the Order Entry Tools' strike prices and choose a different one from the menu. Then the debit or credit resulting from that will appear. It is a quick way to assess verticals to find out if one is appropriate for you.

- Fire up the platform of Thinkorswim.

- Enter a symbol from the trade tab.

- Choose to display the Prob OTM column in the Options Chain, a theoretical number indicating the probability that the inventory will be above the strike price of the short put at expiration. There is no assurance that the OTM option will expire. But to help begin your selection process, it's a metric.

- Next, discover a put strike price that may have between 65 percent and 70 percent Prob. OTM.

- Select that, choose Sell, then Vertical. (See the sidebar "Ways to Place a Vertical Spread" to place a vertical spread order.) Look at the credit for the short vertical spread created in the section Order Entry. A target credit that is one-third the difference between the strike prices is one strategy to consider (i.e., 0.33 credit for a short 46/47 put vertical, 0.66 credit for a short 45/47 vertical, 1.66 credit for a 42/47 vertical, etc.). To see if the resulting credits meet that one-third target, you can adjust the short put up and down strike. But be careful not to choose a set that is too close to the price of the stock. It may not give enough room for the stock to drop some and still allow the short vertical to be profitable.

What Strikes do you Want to Trade?

You can think about putting a vertical spread once you've selected the strikes. Chart source: from TD Ameritrade, the thinkorswim® platform. Only for illustrative purposes.

It's up to you to determine appropriate credit for a short put vertical as an options trader. If you don't find short spreads that give you a one-third credit, this is an indication that you might want to consider debit spreads-a bullish long vertical call in this case. Start by looking for the first in-the-money (ITM) strike, the long call. Select it, click Buy, then click Vertical. For the long vertical call that is generated in the Order Entry segment, look at the debit. Changing the short call strike to the first OTM strike, if possible. One thing to look after is to see if the debit is inferior to the long call's intrinsic value. If the stock worth is $50, and the long 49/51 call's vertical debit is 0.90, it is 0.10 less than the long 49 call's $1 intrinsic value. For ITM options only, inherent value exists.

If the debt is lower than the intrinsic value, if the stock price remains where it is, the vertical will 'grow' into the inherent value at expiration. The benefit will be the difference between the long Vertical's intrinsic value and debit. Again, you opt to pay for a lengthy vertical on the required debit. One benchmark you calculate could be debit versus inherent value.

This method of finding credit or debit verticals as speculative instruments, powered by IV percentiles, teaches you to measure them. There's no guarantee that it would produce successful trades to find verticals this way. But at the very least, it's a way for you to compare debit and credit spreads, or two or more debit spreads, or two or more credit spreads. You can also reach verticals between different underlying structures and learn to calculate their relative possibilities.

So go ahead and change the IV percentile goals, chance, debits, credits, and attacks. But make it an organized, knowledgeable process that you can efficiently and effectively replicate.

Knowing the Difference Between Straddle Vs. A Strangle:

Straddle Vs. Strangle: A Review

Straddles and strangles are options strategies that allow an investor, whether the stock moves up or down, to benefit from significant fluctuations in a stock price. Both methods consist of purchasing an equal number of calls and presenting alternatives of the same expiration date. The difference is that there are two different strike prices for the strangle, whereas there is a similar strike price for the straddle.

Options are a type of derivative protection, which means that the options' price is intrinsically related to someone else's cost. You have the right, but not the duty, to buy or sell an underlying asset at a fixed price on or before a specific date if you buy an option contract.

A call option offers an investor the right to purchase stock, and the right to sell a stock is granted to an investor by a put option. An option contract's strike price is when an underlying stock may be purchased or sold. Before a trade can be exercised for a benefit, the stock must rise above this price for calls or fall below for puts.

Straddle

A straddle consists of buying or selling the same strike with both a call and a put. It is generally achieved with at-the-money options. As at-the-money calls and puts have about 50 deltas, positive and negative, respectively, it is initially a delta neutral strategy. You buy the call for a long straddle and position it, and you sell them for a short straddle.

Long Straddle

- They are long gamma, long vega, and negative Theta with a long straddle. You are investing cash, purchasing premium, by buying both the call and the put. It would help if you had inventory to shift dramatically in either direction and to boost implied volatility, both before too much time passes. Your upside and downside benefit potential is infinite (until the stock hits zero) and what you paid for the straddle is your maximum loss.

- If you have purchased a straddle near expiration, the time decay on the options' premium would be severe. Therefore, you would need inventory to go either up or down beyond the straddle's price to make money. To make up for the time decay, a step up in implied volatility might or may not be enough. If you think the stock's change, up or down, would be more significant than the straddle price, you could purchase a near-term straddle before a case. With this approach, it is essential to look at historical trends after events. For example, if it's earnings, you might look at the previous three or more earnings to see if the stock has moved since the announcement above the straddle price. The average earnings change is also already priced into the options. That's why this approach takes some confidence and accuracy in what you predict. As implied volatility would generally come in, you will also typically want to sell the straddle quickly after the case.

- If you think the stock would pass around a lot over the straddle's lifespan, you might purchase with the intention of scalping stock. The straddle will become a long delta place as inventory goes up (the call goes in-the-money, the put out-of-the-money), and you can sell inventory to remain delta neutral. You become short deltas when the underlying moves down (the put goes in-the-money and the call out-of-the-money), and you'd buy stock to be delta neutral. You will be scalping inventory for a profit with swings up and down.

- Less negative Theta and more positive Vega would have a long straddle further out. Suppose you think that volatility is trading particularly low and that there might be price movement or uncertainty happening down the road that would trigger implied volatility to increase. In that case, one might buy a long straddle a few months out.

- Let's say you're considering a three-month straddle. You could look at 90-day historical volatility to make a volatility decision. A year-long graph of 30-day implied volatility may be another factor. If volatility implied for

30 days was not below, say 40 all year, and you buy lower than that, then you might consider it inferior. About the straddle, you might look at where earnings and events fall and what implied volatility has done historically about earnings and events. The volatility of the underlying against other comparable underlying elements or the market as a whole may be considered.

- While a long straddle would appear to be a low-risk approach, you can see that it needs a lot of thought and consistency of expectation to be profitable.

Short Straddle

On the other side, a high-risk location is a short straddle. As you can see from the graph, there are infinite losses and maximum profits at a price earned for the Straddle sale. Profits are the price of the straddle from the strike only in the period of up or down.

They are short gamma, short Vega, and positive Theta with a short straddle. You want the inventory to remain still, implied volatility to come in, and the premium option to only decline. If you think the implied volatility is exaggerated relative to the movement you expect in the inventory, you might sell a straddle. In general, we will not be discussing trades on the web that include naked short straddles. Still, we might consider in a situation where a trader already has a stock position or was as part of a multi-tier strategy; we do a short straddle as Dan went into PCLN earnings in February 2012.

Strangle

Strangles have many of the same features as straddles, but with a more significant error margin. You buy or sell an out-of-the-money call and an out-of-the-money placed on the same expiration for a stranglehold. The premium charged or earned is therefore significantly lower than a straddle. On the other hand, you need the stock to shift slightly with a long strangle or volatility to go up quite a bit more (Vega is smaller out-of-the-money) for it to be profitable. A short strangle has a greater profitability area, but since the premium earned for out-of-the-money options is smaller, the overall benefit is not as high. The Theta is also lower, so decay is not going to be as drastic.

If you believe there is a chance stock that could make a significant jump, you might put on a long strangle, but your confidence is not high enough to pay the premium for a straddle.

Compared to straddles, it can be a lower premium strategy, but the risk of losing any of your premia is also higher. If you think volatility is low, if you are right, you can buy a straddle that has a higher chance of being profitable, but if the stock takes an extreme jump, the strangle has a far higher payoff. Your decision will rely on your hopes, your tolerance for risk, and your conviction.

To merit perceived mispricing of options, both straddles and strangles are strategies where the investor assumes that implied volatility or premium does not reflect what the underlying would do but with no clear directional opinion. Often, they are enticing but certainly should be used with consideration. The dangers of short straddles and strangles are evident, but it can also be incredibly tortuous to slow death by decay.

CHAPTER FOUR

GUIDE TO ADVANCED OPTIONS

STRATEGIES

Before continuing, we must emphasize that options reflect a form of investment at a higher level and carry a much higher risk level. As such, investors are encouraged to fully understand and learn how to trade options before investing and invest only in venture capital.

An individual must obtain a copy of the Features and Risks of Standardized Options before purchasing or selling an option (ODD). Copies of the ODD are available from your broker, by calling 1-888-OPTIONS, or from One North Wacker Drive, Suite 500, Chicago, Illinois 60606, The Options Clearing Company.

This guide assumes you are already a fundamental understanding of option trading fundamentals, such as buying and selling calls and puts. Check out our Options Basics Guide if you want to learn about the fundamentals of options trading. In essence, any option strategy comes down to a combination of buying and selling calls and placing options at different strike prices and expiry dates, no matter how complicated they are. Other variations of these basic building blocks of options trading are used to suit the investor's risk profile and market outlook.

On a particular stock, are you bullish, neutral, or bearish? Are you willing to gamble more or prefer a more cautious approach? Do you like to monitor your trades regularly or purchase a spot and wait until expiration? There's an option plan for you, whatever your interests are. Some of the more advanced choices, such as butterflies and iron condors, will be covered in this guide.

Bullish Option Tactics

This page's strategies are bullish because if the underlying stock goes up in price, the maximum benefit is received. These trades are typically put shortly with an expiration date. The underlying inventory would then need to go up in the short term.

However, you can open a trade with a longer expiration date, but the options become more costly because of the options' higher time value. For the businesses to break even and become profitable, this would cause these trades to be less profitable or enable the underlying stocks to increase in price by a greater amount.

To see more detailed explanations and examples, click the links for each technique.

Call Backspread

Buying two out-of-the-money calls and selling one in-the-money call generates a Call Backspread, giving you a net credit premium. It is intended for stocks that are bullish and extremely volatile. If the stock climbs, you receive an infinite bonus. You get to retain the original net credit premium if the stock falls. You will take a loss if the stock price does not move.

Covered Call

First, by purchasing or holding on to an existing underlying stock, a covered call is formed. A call option that is either at-the-money or only out-of-the-money, receiving an initial premium, is then sold or "write."

If the price of the underlying stock ends below the strike price of the call option at the expiry date, you will hold the original premium as well as the underlying stock. To receive the compensation each month, you should keep doing this. However, if the underlying stock price ends up above the call option's strike price, you are called out and must sell the stock at the strike price. As well as any capital gains from selling the stock, you receive the original premium.

Married Put

The Married Put position is a form of insurance or hedging to protect your investment in the underlying stock. It is generated by buying the underlying stock at any strike price of your choosing and purchasing the related put option. How likely and how much you think the stock price is expected to fall will depend on the number of put options and the strike price. You would be offered more cover by purchasing more options and at a lower strike price. However, because of the higher fee charged for the option premiums, this insurance comes at an increased initial expense.

The Long Stock Synthetic

Call and Put Synthetics requires the acquisition and sale of a call at the same strike price or vice versa. A Synthetic Long Stock is a bullish approach that needs the purchasing and sale of a market. If the stock price climbs, it has infinite profit and unlimited loss if the stock price falls. Since options are offered, it is essential to close this role before expiration.

Neutral Non-Volatile Option Strategies

This page's strategies are neutral as if the underlying stock does not change much in price; the maximum benefit is obtained. These trades are typically put shortly with an expiration date. The underlying stock price would, therefore, need to stay stable in the short run.

While the underlying stock price will fluctuate a little, these neutral strategies enable the stock price to remain within a non-moving trading range.

To see more detailed explanations and examples, click the links for each technique.

Spread Call Ratio

A Call Ratio Spread is a technique involving buying one in-the-money call and selling two at-the-money calls with very little initial outlay. It is a neutral strategy for stocks with low volatility. If the stock price doesn't move, you hit full profit. When the stock price rises so high, you suffer limitless losses.

Long Butterfly

Buying an in-the-money call, selling two at-the-money calls, and buying an out-of-the-money call requires a long butterfly. It is a neutral, low-risk strategy for stocks with low volatility. If the stock doesn't move much, you gain full minimal income. If the stock rises too high or falls too low, you will incur maximum restricted losses.

Iron Butterfly

A long iron butterfly is a credit position and includes opening a call spread (selling at-the-money call and purchasing out-of-the-money call) and a put spread (sell at-the-money put and buy out-of-the-money put). It is a neutral low-risk strategy for low volatility stocks. If the stock doesn't move, you reach the maximum limited profit. If the stock rises too high or falls too low, you will incur maximum restricted losses.

Iron Condor

The creation of an out-of-the-money bearish call spread and an out-of-the-money bullish put spread is a Long Iron Condor. It is a neutral, low-risk strategy for stocks with low volatility. If the stock price stays within a price range, you retain limited credit revenue. When the stock climbs too high or falls too low, you will incur narrow losses.

Set Ratio Spread

A Put Ratio Spread has very few initial costs and is generated by buying one in-the-money put and selling two in-the-money puts. It is ideal for non-volatile stocks that are neutral. If the stock price doesn't move, the maximum profit is achieved. When the stock price falls too low, unlimited losses are incurred.

Short Strangle

For stocks that do not change much, a short stranglehold is a neutral strategy. It is created by selling an out-of-the-money call and selling an out-of-the-money with the same expiration date. It offers an initial credit premium, which, if the stock stays within the two strike rates, would be your benefit. Losses may be infinite if the stock rises or falls below these strike rates.

Volatile Option Strategies

The strategies are unpredictable because if the underlying stock price changes a lot, whether up or down, the maximum benefit is obtained. These trades are typically put shortly with an expiration date. In the short term, the underlying stock price would also need to move a lot.

To see more detailed explanations and examples, click the links for each technique.

The Long Strangle

A Long Strangle is a high volatility stock strategy but whose course is unclear. It is generated with the same expiration date by purchasing an out-of-the-money call option and an out-of-the-money put option. If the inventory increases or falls, future earnings are infinite. You lose the premium spent on this position if the stock price doesn't move.

Short Butterfly

Selling an in-the-money call, buying two at-the-money calls, and selling an out-of-the-money call includes a short butterfly. It is a strategy in a position that is strong in volatility but neutral. It is a place of credit. When the stock rises or falls, you make little money. When the stock doesn't move much, you incur losses.

Short Iron Butterfly

The debit place is a short iron butterfly that is heavy in volatility but neutral in position. By buying an at-the-money (ATM) call and selling an out-of-the-money call, along with buying an at-the-money put and selling an out-of-the-money put, it is produced. If the stock price does not move, you suffer maximum losses and achieve maximum restricted benefit when the stock price moves a ton.

Short Iron Condor

A Short Iron Condor is opened by establishing an out-of-the-money bullish call spread and an out-of-the-money bearish set spread. If the stock price moves a lot, it is a strategy that is high in volatility but balanced in direction, giving you limited gains and limited losses if the stock price does not rise. For this benefit profile, there are other, more optimal strategies.

Straddle

With similar expiration dates and strike rates, you buy both a Call and a Put in a Straddle strategy for the same stock. This approach is useful for stocks where volatility is predicted, but you don't know which way it will go. If the stock jumps or falls, you can benefit.

Variety of Options for Trading

Here are the various kinds of options:

1. Naked calls and puts.
2. Call credit spreads.
3. Put credit spreads.
4. Call debit spreads.
5. Put debit spreads.
6. Covered calls.
7. Iron condors & butterflies.
8. Straddles & strangles.
9. Calendar spreads.

Different kinds of approaches to choices yield different outcomes. Starting with the easy options is necessary and working your way through the more complicated strategies.

1. Spreads

Spreads are the types of options that form the basis of a variety of strategies for options. They provide better security than naked calls and puts, as well.

Spreads, in reality, limit risk. Nevertheless, they restrict profit as well. That isn't always a bad thing, though. Particularly with the Greeks and the various moving parts of the agreement on options.

There are vertical spreads you'll find in your broker's options chain. If you want a debit spread or a credit spread, you can decide.

They've got multiple targets. As a consequence, with a goal in mind, you need to go in. That will help you determine which types of spread options you want to trade or if you wish to use a spread to build a different strategy for options.

2. Straddles and Strangles are types of options

Straddles and strangles are other kinds of techniques for alternatives. If the stock goes up or down dramatically, they both allow you to make money.

Both types of options require the same number of calls to be purchased and the same expiry date to be placed. The distinction between the two types of options is that there are two different strike prices for a strangle, whereas a straddle has the same strike prices.

It could be a positive form of exchange in terms of earnings. You don't know if the sales will be good or bad; You'd trade a straddle as a result. You would benefit if the stock went up or down dramatically.

For example, you have chosen to buy XYZ stock on earnings. You have agreed to purchase the Can call and place the strike price at $15. The call costs $3, and the installment costs $2. The exchange will cost you $500 in total. $3+$2=$5 and note that 100 shares are owned by one deal, so you'd multiply that by 100 to get $500.

Straddle benefits because both a call and a put are owned so that you make money in whatever way you want. It's important to note, however, that one of the contracts is going to be lost.

As a result, you will need the advice to transfer more than $3 to benefit. Although there is no directional bias from a straddle, a strangle does. With a stranglehold, you assume that stock would shift in a specific direction.

However, to cover yourself, you buy the opposite deal. Straddles are less costly and do not require such a big step to break even.

3. Iron Condors Are Types of Options

Remember how we said there had been different alternatives to make money in any market? Iron condors are a strategy to make money in an impartial market.

It isn't pleasant when stock market trading starts hitting those scope trading days or weeks. Nothing seems to be hitting the stock detectors, and the warehouse near is trying to find plays.

It is where the iron condor gets involved. It is a limited threat of non-directional plays. They do best when there's low volatility.

An iron condor is a mixture of spreads. For example, a bull put distributed and a bear call spread.

Study and Practice

The different types with options strategies were established for our protection. But you need to put in the effort to research them. Most new traders dive straight into options without an understanding of what makes an option tick.

We can't emphasize the significance of the practice of trading them enough for you. That will be the difference between a loss and a benefit. Open an account that is simulated. TD Ameritrade at ThinkorSwim is a fantastic one.

When you learn how to trade various forms of options, you open up an entirely new way to make money while protecting yourself without putting up a lot of cash. Take our FREE options trading courses to get a full idea of the world of advanced options and various forms.

How to Read A Table of Options?

With more details available and the ability to trade online options rapidly, investors are getting savvier using a mix of ETFs, options, and other assets to speculate, hedge, and build their financial strategies. Options are financial instruments that fluctuate, such as an ETF, based on an underlying asset. Multiple factors decide the option's value, including the length of time before the option expires, the volatility of the underlying asset, and the proximity of the strike price of the option to the cost of the underlying asset. Option pricing models also provide the "Greeks" values used to decide how the underlying asset and option price are related. Learning to read a table of options will provide more insight into these principles and how they contribute to the meaning of options.

The (CBOE) Chicago Board Options Exchange, the exchange in which options are exchanged, is the primary source for options pricing and statistics.

Option Table Explained Description

Just below the ETF price, with a set of dates following it, we see "View by Expiration." Figure 1 shows option prices for May

2013, as shown by "May 13" being picked. If you wish to see that expire in a specific month, you can select them from the list, keeping in mind that the month represents the expiry month and that the number after that represents the expiry year. For example, selecting "Jan 15" will display options that expire in January 2015 [see 13 ETFs Every Trader Options Must Know].

First of all, Yahoo! Finance lists call options, followed by put options. To see Put Options' price, scroll down the page until you see the Put Options section.

Strike (Price): This column shows the price at which, if the option is exercised, a call buyer can purchase the defense. In the situation of a put option, if the option is exercised, it's the price at which the option holder will sell the underlying security. On the flip side, when an option he or she sells (writes) is exercised, an option writer will be assigned to deliver the underlying security at the strike price.

The SPY closed at $166.94 on that day, so options with a strike price close to $167 were very successful—a quote from a SPY call option with a $167 strike.

Symbol: This options table feature contains the details you're looking at for which option; it can be broken down into a few main parts.

Last: the price of the previous exchange that passed.

Chg (Change): Change is how much has changed from the previous close, the last price.

Bid: The price at which buyers attempt to purchase the option. If you sell an option on the market, you will usually get this amount, assuming immediate execution. For one share, this is the price. Because one option is for 100 shares, you must multiply this cost by 100 to get an option.

Ask: The price the vendors are trying to sell the option at. If you buy an option on the market, you will usually get this price, assuming immediate execution. For one share, this is the price. Because one option is for 100 shares, you must multiply this cost by 100 to get an option.

Volume: Helps you to know how many contracts were traded during the session. When more traders are trying to get in and out of positions, options that have vast volumes usually have a tighter Bid-Ask range.

Open Int (Interest): The number of open contract positions that have not been offset yet.

CHAPTER FIVE

OPTION PRICING MODELS

Option Pricing Models are mathematical models that measure the theoretical value of an option using certain variables. A calculation of what the investment should be worth using all known inputs is the potential value. In other terms, we are given a reasonable value of an option-by-option pricing model. Finance practitioners may change their trading strategies and portfolios, knowing the estimation of an option's fair value. Option pricing models are also essential tools for finance practitioners engaged in the trading of options.

It is also possible to identify alternatives according to their exercise time:

- Only at the expiration date can European style options be exercised.
- It is possible to exercise American style options at any time between the date of purchase and expiration.

The classification mentioned above is hugely relevant because our choice of option pricing model would be influenced by choosing between European-style or American-style options.

Risk-neutral Chance

We should understand the idea of risk-neutral probabilities, which are commonly used in option pricing and can be used in various option pricing models before discussing multiple option pricing models.

The risk-neutral likelihood is a theoretical expectation of risk-adjusted potential outcomes. Behind this definition, there are two main assumptions:

1. The actual value of an asset is equal to the discounted risk-free rate of its anticipated payoff.

2. There are no prospects for arbitrage in the market.

The risk-neutral likelihood is the probability that in a risk-neutral environment, the stock price will increase. However, neither do we believe that all market participants are risk-neutral nor that volatile assets can receive a risk-free return rate. The probability of purchasing and selling the assets is determined by this statistical value as if there was a single probability for anything on the market.

Binomial Option Pricing Model

Using a binomial choice pricing model is the best way to price the options. The concept of entirely practical economies is used in this model. Under this assumption, the model will price the Option at each point of a given time frame.

We consider that the underlying asset's price will go up or down in the timeframe under the binomial model. Given the possible costs of the underlying asset and the Option's strike price, in these scenarios, we can determine the payout of the Option, then discount these payoffs and, as of today, find the value of that Option.

Black-Scholes Model

Another widely used option pricing model is the Black-Scholes model. The economists Fischer Black and Myron Scholes discovered this model in 1973. For their discovery, both Black and Scholes won the Nobel Memorial Prize in economics.

The Black-Scholes model was primarily developed for pricing European stock options. Under some assumptions about the distribution of the stock price and the economic climate, the model operates. The assumptions regarding the distribution of stock prices include:

- Over time, continually compounded returns on the inventory are typically distributed and separate.
- The variance of returns that are continuously compounded is known and constant.
- Potential dividends are remembered (as a dollar amount or as a fixed dividend yield).

The Economic Environment Assumptions are:

- The risk-free rate is understood and constant.
- No transaction costs or taxes are available.
- Short-selling at no expense and borrowing at a risk-free rate is feasible.

Nevertheless, if necessary, these assumptions can be relaxed and adjusted for particular conditions. We could easily use this model to price asset options other than stocks (currencies, futures).

In the Black-Scholes model, the primary variables used include:

- **The price of the underlying asset (S)** is the actual asset market price.
- **The strike price (K)** is a price at which you can exercise an option.
- **Volatility (σ)** is an indicator of how far in subsequent periods security prices can move. Volatility in the option pricing model is the most challenging input since historical volatility is not the most accurate model.
- **The time before expiration (T)** is between the measurement and the exercise date of an option.
- **Interest rate (r)** is an interest rate.
- **Dividend yield (δ)** was not the primary input into the model initially. For pricing options on non-paying

dividend stocks, the initial Black-Scholes model was created.

We can derive the following mathematical formulas from the Black-Scholes model to measure the fair value of the European calls and puts:

The above formulas use probabilities modified for risk. N(d1) is the risk-adjusted likelihood of obtaining the stock based on the contract finishing in the money at the Option's expiry. The risk-adjusted likelihood that the Option will be exercised is N(d2). Using the normal cumulative distribution of factors d1 and d2, these probabilities are determined.

The Black-Scholes model is primarily used to measure the potential value of European-style options. Because of their features to be exercised before the maturity date, it cannot be extended to American-style options.

Simulation by Monte-Carlo

Another option pricing model we will consider is the simulation of Monte-Carlo. A more sophisticated way to value options is the Monte-Carlo simulation. This methodology simulates possible future stock prices and then uses them to find the anticipated discounted payoffs for options.

We will address two scenarios in this article: simulation with several cycles in the binomial model and simulation in continuous time.

Scenario 1

Under the binomial model, when the asset (stock) price goes up or down, we consider the variants. In the simulation, our first step is the assessment of the stock price's growth shocks. It can be accomplished using the following formulas:

The length of a time is h in these formulas, and $h = T/N$ and N is a sequence of periods.

We will find the Option payoff and discount this payoff to the present value after finding future asset prices for all required periods. To get more reliable results, we need to replicate the previous steps many times and then combine all the present values found to find the Option's fair value.

Scenario 2

There is an infinite number of time points in continuous time from two points in time. Hence, at each point in time, each variable carries a specific value.

We will use the Geometric Brownian Motion of the stock price under this scenario, which means that a random walk follows the stock. Random walking suggests that past patterns do not forecast future stock prices because the price shifts are independent of each other.

We may specify the formula for the stock price shift in the Geometric Brownian Motion model:

$$\Delta S = S(\mu \Delta t + \sigma \varepsilon \sqrt{\Delta t})$$

Where:

t – *Time*

ΔS – *Change in stock price*

S – *Stock price*

σ – *Standard deviation of stock returns*

μ – *Expected return*

$\square$ – *Random variable μ*

In the continuous-time simulation, we do not need to simulate each cycle's stock price, unlike the simulation in a binomial model. Still, we need to calculate the stock price at maturity, S (T), using the following formula:

$$S(T) = S_0 e^{((r-\delta-0.5\sigma^2)T + \sigma\varepsilon\sqrt{T})}$$

The random number is generated, and we solve for S (T). Afterward, the method is similar to what we did in the binomial model for simulation: find the Option payoff at maturity and discount it to the present value.

Recognizing ITM, ATM, and OTM

ITM, ATM, and OTM meanings

In-the-money ITM.

At-the-money ATM.

Out-of-money OTM.

It is the meaning of these sentences in brief and what they say. To effectively trade binary options contracts, you need to understand each of these definitions, what they mean in practice, and the various potential consequences when you place an order. This article will help you understand the value of ITM, ATM, and OTM as a contract so that you can make more educated trading decisions.

What is In-the-money (ITM)?

When the indicative market is overhead the strike by at least one tick or point, a binary option contract is in-the-money.

If you buy binary option contracts, ITM contracts are the most likely to make you a profit. It is because three forms to benefit are available:

- It keeps going up the indicative price.

- The market remains flat.
- The price of the indicative goes down but remains above the strike.

The key drawback is the higher bid/offer price when purchasing ITM binary option contracts. It is because the deal is already in-the-money, and the probability of benefit is greater.

Owing to this higher bid/offer price, you would have a lower profit potential. The benefit is often measured out of $100 for binary options contracts, so the profit potential would be smaller if you have paid more for the contract. For instance, your profit potential is $30 ($100 - $70) if you spend $70 on an ITM contract. Your profit potential is $70 if you pay $30 for the deal. Except for taxes, benefit potential is estimated.

Below is an example of a ticket for an ITM order. The strike price is 1734.5, as you can see, and the underlying market is at 1743.907, which is higher than the strike price. The bid/offer prices would be above the $50 mark if you were to purchase this contract, restricting your potential benefit. However, if you assume that this market will return, passing the strike level of 1734.5, you will look to sell this contract, and your profit potential will be more significant, reflecting the increased risk of this trade.

What is At-the-money (ATM)?

It is said that the binary option contract, which is nearest to the strike price, is at-the-money. It is generally priced at about $50, as it is equally likely to become an ITM or OTM. Generally, there is only one binary choice agreement known as ATM, though there may be others that are OTM and ITM. About the payout conditions, be mindful that a binary option contract cannot expire at-the-money. As the problem is expressed as more significant than in the binary options strike, it must be one tick or point above the strike to be labeled ITM. If it is not greater than but precisely equal to the strike price, then from a payout perspective, it is called OTM (except Nadex Events contracts where it is greater than or equal to the strike price to settle ITM). It is essential to note that this is near to expiration - one tick will make all the difference to the contract settlement.

We have a binary options agreement in this instance that can be known as an ATM, as the strike price of 1744.5 is nearest to the indicative underlying price of 1743.860. Both buyers and sellers have a very similar cost to reward ratios due to this proximity.

What is Out-of-the-Money mean (OTM)?

When the current market is below the strike price, a binary option contract is out-of-the-money. Those who sell the contract (i.e., those who agree that at expiration, the current market will be below the strike price) are more likely to make a profit.

We can see that the 1754.50 strike price is higher than the 1743.07 underlying indicative demand on the order ticket below. A trader selling the contract could benefit in three ways in this case:

- The underlying sector is heading lower.
- The demand underlying it remains the same.
- The underlying market goes up, then expires at or below the 1754.50 strike point.

The bid/offer rates are, as you can see, below the $50 mark, restricting your potential profit if you were to sell this contract. However, if you assume that this market will revert and shift in the opposite direction, passing the 1754.50 strike stage, you will look to purchase this contract. Your profit potential will be higher, reflecting this trade's additional risk.

Examples of ITM, ATM, and OTM Binary Option

Here is an example to explain the different potential consequences, depending on whether ITM, ATM, or OTM, for a binary choice contract.

You can see in this picture that 1743.367 is the indicative price for gold. Below the different strike prices are specified. They fell into three classifications:

- **ITM.** There are contracts where the strike price is below the indicative underlying market (i.e., below 1743.367)- in the lower portion of the picture, you can see them. Take the >1737.0 strike as an example. The response to the question "will the strike be above 1737.0" is already "yes," which is why ITM is the contract. If you are a buyer, the in-the-money agreements offer you the highest potential to benefit. It also suggests that they would be the most costly to purchase.

- **ATM.** As seen in the center of the picture above, this is the strike nearest to the indicative price of 1743.367 (1743.0). At this point, there is an equal probability that the market will move above or below the strike. So the bid and offer prices of the contract will be closest to $50. Note, only one strike is called an ATM strike.

- **OTM.** When the underlying demand is below the strike price, a contract is OTM. It applies, as they are higher than 1743.367, to the top four strikes in the picture. ITM is less likely to conclude these deals and to be profitable for consumers. As a result, buyers are typically priced lower; sellers who have the statistical advantage will pay more for these contracts.

Fundamental Vs. Technological Evaluation

Thanks to the innovation in charting packages and trading platforms, technical analysis is becoming an increasingly common trading approach. However, technical understanding analysis and how it can help forecast developments can be overwhelming and difficult for a novice trader.

The study of price movements in a market is a technical analysis, whereby traders use historical chart patterns and indicators to forecast future market trends. It is a visual representation of a market's past and present output. It enables the trader to use this knowledge before entering a trade-in price action, indicators, and patterns to guide and warn future trends.

This tutorial for beginners in technical analysis will introduce you to this trading method's fundamentals and how it can trade in the financial markets.

The identification of patterns from charts requires technical research. Traders use historical data, mainly based on price and volume, and use this data to detect trading opportunities based on common market trends. Various metrics are added to graphs to evaluate entry and exit points for traders to optimize trades' potential at good risk-reward ratios. Though essential analysis advocates agree that economic forces are the key contributors to market movements, traders in technical analysis maintain that historical patterns may help forecast potential price movements. Since these trading styles can vary, it can be advantageous to understand the differences between fundamental and technical analysis and incorporate them.

Many traders have found the technical analysis of a valuable risk management technique and can be a crucial stumbling block. It can be applied to every market once a trader understands the concepts and technical analysis principles, making it a versatile analytical method. Where basic analysis seeks to identify inherent market value, the technical analysis aims to identify patterns that can be easily induced by the underlying fundamentals.

The advantages of the use of technical research include:

- Can be extended using any timeline to any sector
- As a standalone tool, technical analysis may be used
- Enables traders to spot business patterns

For technical analysis, charts are key. The price itself is the most relevant indicator of the past and present success of a market; this is the point of departure when evaluating a trade's potential. As this is the clearest indicator of what the market is doing, price action can be depicted on a map.

Charts help assess the overall trend over the long or short term, whether there is an upward or downward trend or defining range-bound situations. Line charts, bar charts, and candlestick charts are the most common kinds of technical analysis charts.

Each duration would give the technical analyst information about the price from where it opened, the high or low of the period, and the closing using a bar or candlestick map. Analysis of candlesticks is instrumental because the trends and relationships inside them can help predict the price's future direction.

When a trader has learned the fundamentals of charting, they may then use indicators to assess the pattern.

Technical Research- Tools Indicators

When searching for opportunities in the market, measures are used by technical traders. While there are many indicators, traders mostly make use of parameters focused on volume and pricing. It helps decides where the levels of support and opposition are, how much they are sustained or broken, and the duration of a pattern is calculated.

Using multiple time frame analysis, a trader may view the price or some other metric, varying from one second to a month, which gives the trader a different viewpoint on the price action.

For technical research, the more common indicators include:

- Moving Averages
- The relative index of strength (RSI)
- Divergence of moving average convergence (MACD)

Technical Research- Model

Transitions between rising and declining trends are also indicated in technical analysis by price patterns. By meaning, a price pattern is a recognizable price movement configuration that is defined using a set of trendlines and curves.

When a price pattern signals changes in trend direction, it is referred to as a reversal pattern; when the trend persists in its current direction after a brief delay, a continuation pattern occurs.

Technical analysts have long used price trends to analyze current movements and predict potential market movements.

Patterns are the distinctive formations formed on a graph by the movements of security prices and are the basis of technical analysis.

A trend is defined over a particular period by a line that crosses common price points, such as closing prices or peaks or lows.

Technical analysts and chartists aim to identify trends to predict the future direction of a security price.

These trends can be as plain as trendlines and as complicated as formations of double head-and-shoulders.

Technical Research trendlines

Since a series of lines and curves are used to define price trends, it is beneficial to understand trendlines and know how to draw them. Trendlines assist technical analysts in spotting support and resistance areas on a price map. Trendlines are straight lines drawn by joining several descending (high) peaks or ascending troughs on a graph (lows).

When prices experience higher peaks and higher lows, a trendline that is tilted up, or an up trendline, exists. By linking the ascending lows, the upward trendline is drawn. Conversely, when prices encounter lower highs and lower lows, a trendline that is bent down, called a down trendline, exists.

Trendlines vary in appearance depending on what part of the price bar is used to "connect the dots." While there are different schools of thought on which part of the price bar should be used, the candle bar body, not the thin wicks above and below the candle body, always represents where most price action has taken place to provide a more valid point.

Chartists also use closing prices on daily charts to draw trendlines rather than peaks or lows, as the closing prices reflect traders and investors willing to keep a place overnight or over a weekend or market holiday. As a general rule, trendlines with three or more points are more valid than those based on only two points.

Uptrends occur when rates generate higher highs and lower lows. At least two of the lows are linked by up trendlines and display support levels below the price.

Downtrends happen when markets generate lower highs and lower lows. At least two of the highs are linked by down trendlines and suggest resistance levels above the price.

Consolidation, or a sideways market, occurs where the price oscillates along with two parallel and sometimes horizontal trendlines between an upper and lower range.

CHAPTER SIX

THE OPEN ROTATION

What is Open Rotation?

The system is used to open trading on an options market is open rotation. During a normal trading day, this process typically takes place for the first time each morning. If trading is stopped in the middle of the day at some stage, the free rotation method can also be used again.

A type of market order can also be referred to by the term free rotation. In this case, it relates to either purchasing or selling option security to remain active throughout the opening trading rotation of a normal trading day. Open orders for a rotation that are not filled during the initial cycle expire immediately.

Understanding Open Rotation

Open rotation in the stock market is equivalent to an at-the-opening order (but an open circuit occurs in the options market). Unlike stocks, before an opening price for the underlying security has been calculated, options must wait to begin trading.

It is achieved by a mechanism that accepts orders and quotations first for the sequence of call options that expire the fastest and have the lowest strike price. In all the near-term series of call options, this rotation continues. Then the cycle goes farther out on the calls that expire.

The process begins with the put options until all of the calls are available, starting with the highest strike price and the nearest expiration date. With lower strike prices, the rotation mechanism then goes on to puts. Eventually, with longer-dated expirations, it passes on to options. Until all option series underlying a specific stock are exchanged on the market, this rotation mechanism continues.

For an entire options sequence, the amount of time it takes to complete the full open rotation depends on the trading volume for both the underlying stock and the options. For stocks with more liquidity, the process appears to move faster. Such stocks often tend to have options with a relatively larger amount of trading; this further speed up the free rotation.

Unique Considerations

An open rotation order doesn't necessarily mean that the order at the opening bell must be executed. During fast market conditions, a rotation can also often come into play if markets are not running in an orderly fashion. When a stock is halted, all trading options on that same stock will also be stopped (until the stock reopens). At this stage, the phase of rotation begins again.

It can also refer to trades conducted when for different reasons, the market opens back up after closing, including technical problems requiring the reopening of midday trading. For example, floor officials on the Chicago Board Options Exchange will stop trading for up to two business days if the underlying stock has a delayed opening or if there are other unusual circumstances.

Open rotation comes back into play once trading returns. Furthermore, during unusual market conditions, the exchange will suspend stop and limit orders to help restore the market's integrity. Again as the market restarts, free rotation is used.

Psychology of Trading: 6 Practical Tips for Mastering the Mind and Money

Get work and quickly solve much of your trading psychology problems; I know that this could sound strange.

But getting a job (or an alternative source of revenue) increases your trading's psychology and performance.

Here is the reason why:

- It reduces the need to make money syndrome.
- It helps you to expand your trading account quickly.

Just let me explain.

It **eliminates the need to make money syndrome**.

The thing is here:

If trading is your only revenue source, you're psychologically putting yourself at a disadvantage because you'll need to make money every month.

It leads you to make bad trading decisions such as expanding your stop loss, averaging losers, trading too big, and that's why many professional traders, as their only source of income, do not rely on trading.

Don't you trust me? Enable me to prove it to you! Ed Seykota, a Business Magician, has a $99/month exchange tribe. A stock market wizard, Mark Minervini, provides a $5,000-cost master trader software.

Even if it's a losing year, most hedge funds (even the best ones) charge a management fee. If you have a billion-dollar hedge fund and take a 2 percent management fee to put it in perspective, it means you get $20 m a year, guaranteed. Professional traders and hedge funds, as you can see, arrange their trading in a way that is not their sole source of revenue.

So, if you wish to level the playing field, what would a retail trader like you do? Easy: getting a job.

You have a basis of income every month if you have a career, no matter what. It enables you to concentrate on trading without thinking about whether you can cover the bills this month.

It helps you to expand your account faster so that you can trade bigger and make more money.

Here is it:

In investing, you need liquidity to make money.

Let's say that 20 percent a year is your average return. It tells you will make around $200 a year on a $1000 account. You will make about $20,000 a year on a $100,000 account. Likewise, you will make around $200,000 a year on a $1m account.

So the issue now is, how can you lift your trading account size? To increase your trading account size, you can use a portion of your revenue (from your job). It implies that you can trade more and make more money and, in my view, getting a full-time job is one of the best things you can do with your trade.

Backtest your approach and gain huge confidence in your trading

Here is it:

Having confidence in your trading strategy is one of the most significant challenges you can face. Think about how you can find the conviction to sell it during a drawdown if your trading strategy does not have an edge in the markets?

Meanwhile, you're going to start searching for the next "best trading tactic" instead, and then the rinse of the loop repeats itself.

You have to have an edge in the markets to break out of the loop to have conviction in your trading strategy.

How do you go about it, then?

It relates to how your trading strategy operates to determine whether it has an edge in the markets with past results. Now, if it is proven that your trading strategy works with past data, then there is a fair chance that it will work in the future, giving you trust in your trading, right?

So here are two ways that you can do that:

1. Backtesting manually
2. Backtesting Systematically

Backtesting manually

It relates to backtesting the solution in a manual manner. You'd swipe through your charts literally and evaluate the business as it unfolds bar by bar.

There are pros and cons.

Pros:

- You do not need any particular expertise.
- You will know how to decipher the price behavior of the markets.

The Cons:

- The findings could not be correct due to hindsight bias.
- You do not understand what the net risk to your portfolio is.

Here's the step by step you can do it.

1. Know the trading configuration you are looking for

You need to know what the setup you're looking for, whether you're trading pullback, breakouts, etc., is before you can do some backtesting.

Then, create a trading strategy so that you can objectively classify your trades.

2. Scroll back to an instrument's earliest starting date

Next, go back to the earliest date on your device that you can get. You will be able to go back a few years on TradingView or MT4 for the standard timeframe.

3. Shift the chart forward one bar at a time and check for your setup for trading

Here's where the fun starts. Imagine the "live markets" in front of your phone, and you're trading in real-time.

It means that it is essential to plot your help & resistance; your related indicators should be on the screen, and so on.

Then as the price unfolds bar by bar, look for your trading setups.

4. Your Trade Publication

You want to record your entry, exit, stop loss, and R multiple once you've established your trading setup.

Till you arrive at the current date, repeat the process. To see if you have an advantage in the markets, collect all the data you have recorded.

Backtesting Systematically

It applies to the systematic process of backtesting your approach using a programming language such as Python, R, etc.

Here are the pros and contras of this strategy:

Pros:

- In minutes, you can backtest your plan.
- You understand what the net risk to the portfolio is.

The Cons:

- You can curve past data that contribute to a strategy that does not succeed in the real world.
- You need knowledge of programming.

Now, my strength field is not systematic backtesting, so I can't tell you how to do it.

But here are some tools that may be of assistance to you:

- Learn how to code for free from **Codeacademy.**
- Premium data provider for your backtesting needs **Norgate.**
- **Amibroker:** strong tools for backtesting.
- **Joemarwood:** A trading blog that shares realistic systematic trading tips and tricks.

You can always employ someone to systematically backtest your method if you do not want to practice.

Using the Star System and maximize the results of your trading

The Star system is a tool I've built to help traders achieve consistent outcomes. However, until I get to it, let me ask you a question; have you ever attempted to use a trading strategy, and you conclude after a few losses that it doesn't fit and start searching for the next best process? It is a massive MISTAKE.

How do you expect a stable set of results if you're always hopping from one trading strategy to the next? It would be impossible!

You need a consistent set of actions to have a consistent set of results.

Let me introduce the Star system that I have created to help traders be consistent in their actions.

Here's how I figured it out:

Remember, when you were in kindergarten and did a good job, your teacher would give you a star-shaped sticker (rewarding you for a job well done).

And this is how it works with the Star system:

- Create a sound trading plan that dictates your entries, exits, management of trade, and risk management.
- You get 1 star every time you follow your plan.
- You get -2 stars each time you have not followed your plan.
- The Star System's objective is to accumulate 100 stars.

If you know, whenever you deviate from your strategy, you get badly penalized. It is to ensure that you wholeheartedly obey the system and nothing else.

Then you have a decent chance of being a reliably successful trader if you can be consistent in your actions.

Why Should You Be Rich?

You instantly think of Ferraris, Mansions, and Hot Chicks when you hear someone talk about traders. In real life (and I'm talking about 0.001 percent type), a tiny percentage of it happens.

Here is it:

You're playing with probability while trading. You'll have months of winning and months of LOSING. You want to save up to survive the hard times and not get blown away during the good times. Be FRUGAL. But if you spend recklessly on the equipment you like, it puts pressure on your own business.

You'll have suggestions like:

- How am I going to pay for my mansion mortgage?
- How can I impress those around me?
- How do I preserve my Ferrari?

It contributes to the need to make money syndrome, as you know (as mentioned earlier). You end up making bad decisions about trading that cause you to blow up your account. The bottom line, trading's goal is to be wealthy, NOT act rich.

The Technique of the Matrix that makes you feel numb about losing trades

Effective trading means adhering to your trading strategy and managing risk for any single transaction. There will be profits and losses, but you will make money over time if you have an advantage in the markets.

Here is it:

Your reasoning gets thrown out the window when you are trading in the Moment, and you are left struggling against your emotions.

You're watching every market tick.

You're thinking of widening the stop loss so that you don't take a loss.

In the event the economy goes against you, you wonder if you can take income now.

That isn't very good if you think about it. You were fussing over a single trade's result when it's unpredictable.

So how in real-time do you suppress these feelings and increase your trading performance?

Ok, let me introduce The Methodology of the Matrix to you.

If you've watched the movie "Matrix," you know that people are wired into the matrix and disconnected from reality. It is what you want to do to separate yourself from your trades' results for your trading.

"Are you following your schedule for trading?"

If the answer is NO, quit the trade immediately and (whether it is a winner or loser) stop trading. Set your stop loss and step away from your terminal if the answer is YES (knowing that you are doing the right thing and your risk is contained).

It is straightforward, but it works. It removes you from the results of your transactions and keeps you focused on executing your strategy.

How the psychological burden of full-time trading can be overcome, even though you have a family to help

I'm not going to say you sell full-time (unless you know what you do) if you have a family to feed. The pressure to make cash is so high that it hurts your performance in trading. You have bills to pay, a loan, and to provide for your children. Still, because of the freedom it brings, no boss to respond to, and no politics to deal with, you might want to trade full time.

If that's you, then here are six practical tips that will help you:

1. Have a partner that works and will support the family full-time.

It's a massive advantage if you have a partner who wholeheartedly supports your trade.

It allows you to concentrate on your trade without worrying about the bills or putting food on the table and removes enormous pressure.

2. Save 12 months of living expenses before the transition takes place

But what if there isn't a partner for you? Yeah, no worries.

You will save enough cash to cover your living expenses for 12 months (and this excludes your trading capital).

It helps you trade in comfort in knowing that your living costs are always taken care of even though you didn't make money this month.

3. Contribute once every six months to household income

Trading is all about chances, and you need time to play for your advantage.

It means you will not make money every month, but you should be profitable, given a long enough timeframe.

So, a solution to this is to contribute once every six months instead of every month to the household income.

4. Conduct part-time employment as an additional source of income to provide

To augment your trading profits, you should take up part-time work.

For instance, tuition giving, waiting, bartending, etc. Essentially, whatever it takes to provide an extra stream of revenue outside of trading.

5. Educate and get compensated by other traders

You can train other traders and get paid for it with your courses or coaching programs.

For instance:

- Perform a live seminar
- Build an online course
- Perform a program for mentorship
- Give private coaching for 1 to 1
- Write newsletters trading

It is a common strategy used by many successful traders, such as Mark Minervini, Andreas Unger, Peter Brandt, etc.

It's only ideal for those that are reliably profitable, though. Don't worry if you aren't, because the next choice is for you.

6. Recommend goods and services that you believe in for trading

I'm sure you now have some trading goods or services you love to use, then why not get paid to use them by referring to other traders?

For instance:

You will advise others to sign up for an account and get a referral fee if you are satisfied with your broker.

Or you can refer others to it and get a referral fee if you enjoy using a specific charting site (like TradingView). Only goods or services you believe in should be linked to and not because you want to make a fast buck. Your spiritual responsibility is that.

CHAPTER SEVEN

STEPS TO BUILDING A WINNING

TRADING PLAN

In industry, there is an old expression that you plan to fail if you fail to prepare. It may sound glib, but individuals, including traders, who are serious about being good should follow those words as though they were written in stone. Ask any trader who makes money regularly, and they are likely to tell you that you have two options:

1) Execute a written plan methodically, or 2) fail.

You are in the minority if you already have a written trading or investment strategy, congratulations. Developing a strategy or technique that works in financial markets requires time, commitment, and analysis. Although there are never any guarantees of success, you have removed one significant roadblock by designing a comprehensive trading strategy.

Avoiding Catastrophe

Trading is a company, so if you want to succeed, you have to treat it as such. It is not a business strategy to read a few books, purchase a charting software, open a brokerage account, and start trading with real money; it is more like a catastrophe formula.

A strategy should be written when trading but subject to reevaluation when the markets are closed with simple indications that are not subject to change. With market conditions, the strategy will change and see changes as the trader's skill level improves. Taking into account personal trading styles and priorities, each trader should write their plan. Using the strategy of someone else does not represent your trading features.

Building the Ultimate Master Plan

No two trading plans are the same, and there are no two merchants precisely alike. Significant variables such as trading style as well as risk tolerance will reflect each approach. What are the other crucial aspects of a solid trading plan? Here are ten that every program should include:

1. Skill Assessment

Are you trading ready? Have you checked your framework by programming it on paper, and are you sure it will run in a live trading environment? Without hesitation, can you follow your signals? Market trading is a battle of giving and take. The real pros are prepared and profit from the rest of the crowd, who typically give money away after expensive errors without a strategy.

2. Preparing mentally

How're you feeling? Did you sleep enough? Do you feel up to the challenge that lies ahead? If you're not able to fight in the market emotionally and physically, take the day off. Otherwise, you risk losing your shirt. If you are frustrated, worried, or otherwise distracted from the task at hand, this is almost sure to happen.

Before the day starts to get them primed, several traders have a market mantra, which they repeat. Build one that will place you in the zone of trading. Also, distractions should be free from your trade area. Note, this is an organization, and distractions can be expensive.

3. Set Level of Risk

On one trade, how much of your portfolio do you risk? It will depend on your style of trading and risk tolerance. The amount of risk will vary, but it should usually range from about 1 percent to 5 percent of your portfolio on a given trading day. That means you get out of the market and stay out if you lose the amount at some point in the day. If things don't go your way, it's easier to take a break and then fight another day.

4. Set goals

Set achievable profit goals and risk/reward ratios before you enter a trade. What is the minimum risk/reward that you are going to accept? If the potential benefit is at least three times greater than the risk, many traders will not take a trade. If your stop-loss is $1 per share, for example, your target should be a profit of $3 per share. Set and reassess weekly, monthly, and annual profit goals in dollars or as a percentage of your portfolio.

5. Doing your homework

Do you check what is going on across the globe before the market opens? Are stocks up or down overseas? Are pre-market S&P 500 index futures up or down? Since futures contracts trade day and night, index futures are the right way of evaluating the mood before the market opens.

What are the remaining economic or earnings details, and when are they due? Post a list in front of you on the wall and determine if you would like to trade ahead of a significant article. Most traders should wait until the report is published to take excessive trading-related risks during unpredictable report reactions. They're not gambling. It is also a risk to trade ahead of a significant study since it is impossible to know how markets will respond.

6. Preparation for Trade

Whatever trading device and software you use, set alarms for entry and exit signals on the charts, mark significant and minor support and resistance levels, and ensure that all movements can be easily seen or identified with a simple visual or auditory signal.

7. Set Rules for Exit

Many traders make the mistake of focusing most of their energy on searching for purchase signs but pay no attention to when and where to exit. Many traders do not sell if they are down because they don't want to make a loss. Get over it, learn to tolerate failures, or as a trader, you won't make it. If your stop is knockout, it means that you've been mistaken. Don't personally take it. Professional traders lose more trades than they gain, but they still make gains by controlling liquidity and limiting losses.

You should be familiar with your exits before you reach a deal. For every exchange, there are at least two potential exits. What's your stop loss first if the trade goes against you? It has to be written. They don't count mental pauses. Second, there should be a profit goal for each business. Sell a portion of your position once you get there, and if you like, you can switch your stop loss on the remainder of your position to the break-even stage.

8. Set Rules for Entry

For a reason, this comes after the tips for exit rules: Exits are far more relevant than entries. "When to signal A fires, and there is a least target at three times as great as my stop loss, and we are at support, then buy X contracts or shares here. A standard entry rule might be worded like this.

Your scheme should be complicated enough to be effective but easy enough to encourage snap decisions to be effective. If you have 20 conditions that need to be satisfied and all are arbitrary, it would be hard (if not impossible) for you to make trades. Computers also make better traders than humans, which may explain why computer programs produce nearly 50 percent of all businesses that now occur on the New York Stock Exchange.

Computers don't have to feel or think good to make a deal. They join if conditions are met. They exit when the trade goes the wrong way or hits a profit goal. After making a few profitable trades, they don't get mad at the market or feel invincible. Each decision is based, not emotion, on probabilities.

9. Keep records of excellent

Many traders who are seasoned and practical are also excellent at record keeping. If they win a trade, they want to know why and how exactly. More importantly, when they fail, they want to know the same thing, so they do not repeat needless errors. Write down information such as goals, the entry, and exit of each trade, the time, level of support and resistance, daily opening range, open and close to the market for the day, and record feedback on why you made the trade and the lessons learned.

To go back and evaluate the profit or loss for a specific system, drawdowns (which are sums lost per transaction using a trading system), average time per trade (which is crucial to measure trade efficiency). Also, other essential factors, you can save your trading records. Compare these variables to a buy-and-hold approach, as well. Know, this is a corporation, and the accountant is you. You want your company to be as profitable and successful as possible.

10. Efficiency Assess

Adding up the benefit or loss after each trading day is secondary to understanding the why and how. In your trading journal, write down your observations so that you can access them later. Remember, there'll always be trades that lose. A trading strategy that wins over the long term is what you want.

Characteristics of A Trader of Good Options

Options are one of the capital markets' most flexible instruments. Their versatility makes it possible for the trader to exploit their position to maximize returns. These products often allow consumers to control risks by using them for hedging or profiting from the market's upside, downside, and sideways movement.

Despite its many advantages, the trading of options carries a considerable risk of loss and is very risky. Not everyone can become a profitable trader of options. It is becoming a good options trader, like any other business needs a specific skill set, personality, and attitude.

1. Be capable of managing risk

Options are high-risk instruments, and understanding how much risk they have at any point in time is crucial for traders. What is trade's maximum downside? Concerning volatility, what is the implicit or explicit position? How much of my money is devoted to trading? These are some of the questions that traders must always hold in their minds.

To monitor risk, traders also need to take appropriate steps. In particular, you can frequently come across loss-making trades if you are a short-term options trader. For instance, if you hold a position overnight because of negative news, your bet could go wrong. At any moment, you need to be able to mitigate the danger of your positions. By restricting their trade size and diversifying into several different trades, some traders do so that all their eggs are not in the same basket.

An options trader has to be an exceptional money manager as well. They need to make wise use of their money. For instance, blocking 90 percent of your capital in a single trade wouldn't be wise. Whatever methodology you follow, it is not possible to neglect risk management and money management.

2. Be Good with Numbers

You still play with numbers when trading in options. What is the volatility that is implied? Is there a choice in cash or out of money? What is this trade break-even? Traders with options always answer these questions. They often refer to the Greek option of their options trades, such as delta, gamma, vega, and theta. A dealer, for example, would like to know if his business is brief gamma.

3. Possess discipline

Options traders must exercise discipline to become effective. It is all part of the field to do a thorough analysis, find opportunities, set up the right exchange, shape, stick to a plan, set targets, and form an exit strategy. Following the herd is a precise instance of deviating from the discipline. Without conducting your analysis, never believe an opinion. You cannot miss your homework and blame your losses on the herd. Instead, you have to formulate an independent trading strategy that works to make it a profitable strategy for options. Although formal education can be correlated with elite traders in the context of higher degrees, it is not generally the case for everyone. But you have to be trained in terms of the business. It takes time for profitable traders to understand the fundamentals and research the market, different situations, various patterns, and how the market operates. They are not typically novices who have taken a three-hour "How to get rich fast trading" trading seminar, but instead, take the time to learn from the market.

4. Be very Patient

Patience is one attribute that traders in all options have. Instead of making a significant win in any market movement, prudent investors can wait for the market to have the right opportunity. You will also see traders sitting idle and watching the market, hoping to enter or leave a deal at the right moment. For amateur traders, the same is not the case. They are impatient, unable to control their thoughts, and they can enter and leave trades easily.

5. Build a Trading Style

Every trader has a different personality and should follow a trading style that matches his or her characteristics. Some traders may be good at day trading, where they buy and sell options to make small profits many times during the day. With position trading, some may be more relaxed, where they shape trading strategies to take advantage of specific possibilities, such as time decay and volatility. And with swing trading, where traders make bets on market change over periods of five to 30 days, some may be more relaxed.

6. Interpret your news

Reading the news, distinguishing hype from fact, and making appropriate decisions based on this information is crucial for traders. With promising news, you will find many traders willing to put their capital into an option, and the next day they will move on to the next big news. It distracts them from understanding broader industry patterns. Many active traders, rather than only running through the top stories in the press, would be frank with themselves and make sound personal decisions.

7. Be an Active Learner

90 percent of options traders will realize losses, the Chicago Board of Trade (CBOT) announced. Profitable traders can learn from their mistakes and apply what they learn in their trading strategies, which distinguishes successful traders from mediocre ones. Elite traders' practice and practice some more before they learn the lessons behind the trade, understand the business economy and see the market's actions as it happens.

The financial markets are changing and developing constantly; you need to understand what is going on and how it all works. You will not only become good at your current trading strategies by being an active learner, but you will also be able to find new opportunities others may not see or may skip over.

8. Be Flexible

You may not stake a claim on the market, but if it is not the kind that suits you, you have to go with the market or quit it. You have to accept that there are losses and that it is likely that you will lose. Acceptance is paramount to comprehension, clarity, and ultimately winning, rather than battling the market.

9. Plan for Your Trades

It is more likely to succeed an options trader who prepares than one who works on instinct and feel. You will position random trades if you don't have a strategy, and ultimately, you will be directionless. On the other side, you are more likely to stick to it if you have a schedule. You will be explicit about what your priorities are and how you plan to accomplish them. You will also know how the losses can be compensated or when to book income. You will see how the strategy worked for you or did not work). All these measures are essential to establish a profitable trading strategy.

10. Maintain Records

Many successful traders in options keep diligent records of their trades. To help you avoid making expensive decisions, keeping proper trade records is an important habit. The past of your trade reports also offers a wealth of data to maximize your chances of success.

Top Mistakes When Dealing in Cheap Options

Without fully knowing the risks, many traders make the mistake of buying cheap options. One where the absolute price is low is an affordable alternative. The actual value is, however, sometimes overlooked.

Such traders confuse an affordable option with a low-priced option. A low-priced option is when the option, compared to its fundamentals, trades at a low price. Rather than merely cheap, it is undervalued. Investing in inexpensive options is not the same as investing in cheap stocks. The former appears to be at greater risk.

Since options are much more unpredictable than stocks, it is an integral part of risk management to obey strict guidelines.

Gordon Gecko famously said, "Greed is good, for lack of a better word." Greed can be a good motivator for profit. However, Greed can tempt even seasoned traders to take unwise risks when it comes to cheap options. Who does not like a big profit with a small investment, after all?

Out-of-the-money options will look like suitable investments combined with short expiration periods. The initial cost is usually smaller, which makes future income higher if the option is fulfilled. Until investing in cheap options, however, it pays to be conscious of these seven common errors.

1. Not Understanding Volatility

Traders of options use implied volatility to gauge whether an option is costly or cheap. The potential fluctuations (probable trading range) is seen using the data points.

Typically, high implied volatility means a bearish market. Perceived risks often push prices higher when there is fear in the marketplace. That correlates with a costly choice. Low implied volatility also means a bullish market.

To compare current implied volatility, historical volatility, which can be plotted on a map, should also be studied carefully.

2. Ignoring Probabilities and Odds

Han Solo said, did not tell me the odds, "but smugglers don't know anything about the trading of options". The industry will not always work according to the patterns shown by the background of the underlying stock. By leveraging money, some traders claim that buying cheap options helps alleviate losses. However, by not adhering to the rules of odds and probabilities, traders can overrate this kind of security. In the end, such an approach could trigger a significant loss. Odds define the likelihood that an occurrence will or will not happen.

Investors should note that for a reason, inexpensive choices are always cheap. The option is priced, rendering to the statistical expectation of the potential of the underlying stock. The value of a contract for out-of-the-money options depends heavily on its expiration date.

3. Wrong Time Frame Collection

More than one with a shorter time frame would cost an alternative with a longer time frame. There is more time left for the stock to travel in the planned direction, after all.

Longer-dated choices are less prone to time decay as well. The appeal of a cheap front-month contract might, sadly, be overwhelming. Simultaneously, if the shares' movement does not meet the requirements for the option acquired, it can be devastating. For specific derivatives traders, it is also mentally hard to manage stock fluctuations over longer timeframes. The value of options will change as stocks go through a typical sequence of ups and downs.

4. Neglecting Analysis of Sentiment

A definite step in the right direction is to observe short interest, analyst ratings, and place behavior. Jesse Livermore, the great speculator, observed that the stock market is never prominent. It is designed to fool people most of the time." It seems spiritual, but it opens up some doors for traders. On one side or another, when sentiment gets too high, significant profits can be made by betting against the herd. Contrary measures can help traders gain an advantage, such as the put/call ratio.

5. To depend on Guesswork

If the stock goes down, up, or sideways when buying options, ignoring fundamental and technical analysis is a significant mistake. The business has traditionally compensated for easy gains. Therefore, technical metrics need to be used, and the underlying stock evaluated to improve timing.

There is a much stronger case than the stock market for market timing in the options market. According to the useful market hypothesis, it isn't easy to make reliable assumptions on where stocks are going. Based on current uncertainty, the Black Scholes option pricing model offers very different prices for similar options. Buyers of options with longer time horizons should boost efficiency by waiting for lower volatility if the efficient market hypothesis is right.

6. Intrinsic meaning and extrinsic value overlooking

Extrinsic value is always the key determinant of a dealer's cost for cheap options, rather than intrinsic value. The extrinsic value would decrease and ultimately hit zero as the expiration of the option approaches. The majority of options expire without value. Purchasing options that start with intrinsic value is the only way to escape this terrible fate. Rarely are such choices cheap.

7. Not using Orders for Stop-Loss

Many cheap options traders are forgoing the security offered by simple stop-loss orders. When it comes to fruition, they choose to retain an option or let it go until it hits zero. Due to the high volatility of options, there is undoubtedly more chance of being stopped-out early. Those with more discipline may instead choose to use a mental stop or an automatic warning. If an alert was only a blip triggered by the occasional lack of liquidity in the options market, it could still be dismissed.

To prevent whipsaw, stop-loss orders for mental or physical options must allow for more significant losses than inventories. When trading options, growth investor William J. O'Neil proposed restricting losses to 20 percent or 25 percent. That is much more than the 10 percent cap for stop-loss orders that many stock traders use.

CHAPTER EIGHT

BROKER

A broker is someone or a firm that works between an investor and a stock exchange as an intermediary. Since securities exchanges accept orders only from individuals or firms that are members of that exchange, the services of exchange members are required by individual traders and investors. Brokers provide the service and are compensated in different ways, either by commissions, fees or by the exchange itself being charged.

Basics from Broker

As well as executing customer orders, brokers will provide analysis, investment plans, and market aptitude for investors. They can cross-sell other financial products and services provided by their brokerage company, such as access to a private customer offering that provides high net worth customers with customized solutions. Only the rich were able to afford a broker in the past to enter the stock market. An explosion of discount brokers was caused by online broking, which allowed investors to trade at a lower cost but without personalized advice.

Discount vs. Brokers Full-Service

On behalf of a customer, discount brokers can conduct several kinds of transactions, for which they charge a reduced fee in the range of $5 to 15 per deal. Their framework for low prices is based on volume and lower costs. They do not offer investment advice, and brokers usually earn a salary rather than a commission. Many discount brokers deliver an online trading platform that attracts a rising number of self-directed investors.

Full-service brokers deliver various services on top of a full range of investment products, including market analysis, investment advice, and retirement planning. To that end, investors should expect their trades to pay higher commissions. Brokers receive fees based on their trading volume and the selling of investment products from the brokerage house. A growing number of brokers, such as managed investment accounts, offer fee-based investment products.

Brokers for Real Estate

A broker is a licensed real estate specialist in the real estate industry who usually represents a property seller. The duties of a broker when working for a seller can include:

- Determination of land market values.

- Listing the property for sale and advertising it.
- Show prospective purchasers the land.
- Client guidance on deals, conditions, and related matters.
- Submitting all offers for consideration by the seller.

Having a real estate broker work for a client is not unusual, in which case the broker is liable for:

- Locate all properties, sorted by price range and requirements, in the desired region of the buyer.
- Preparation of an original offer and purchase agreement for a buyer who wishes to make a property offer.
- Negotiate on the buyer's behalf with the seller.
- Overseeing land inspections and negotiating fixes.
- Help the buyer to close down and take possession of the land.

Control on Brokers

Brokers registered with the Financial Industry Regulatory Authority (FINRA), the self-regulatory body of a broker-dealer. Brokers are kept to a standard of conduct based on the 'suitability rule' in representing their customers, allowing there to be fair grounds for endorsing a particular product or investment. The second section of the legislation, generally referred to as "know your customer," or KYC, discusses the steps that a broker must take to define their customer and their savings objectives, allowing them to determine the reasonable reasons for the recommendation. The broker must make a reasonable attempt to collect details on the client's financial position, tax status, investment targets, and other information used in making a recommendation.

This conduct level varies significantly from the standard applicable to financial advisors licensed as Registered Investment Advisers with the Securities and Exchange Commission (SEC) (RIAs). RIAs are kept to a strict fiduciary obligation under the Investment Advisors Act of 1940 to always act in the client's best interest while providing full disclosure of their fees.

In the United States, real estate brokers are licensed by each state, not by the federal government. Each state has its laws specifying the kinds of relationships between customers and brokers that may occur and brokers' responsibilities to customers and public members.

Example Real World of Brokers

Several businesses registered with FINRA as brokers, although some can use their classification as brokers for different purposes than others. Many proprietary trading companies are licensed as brokers to access exchanges directly but do not provide broker services to customers as a whole. It varies from the place full-service or discount brokers could have.

Full-service brokers and many other retirement planning services or wealth management prefer to use their position as a brokerage as an ancillary service available to high-net-worth customers. For instance, offers from a company such as Morgan Stanley or Goldman Sachs, or even Bank of America Merrill Lynch may include examples of a full-service broker. These companies can also use their broker services to make big block stock trades on behalf of themselves or corporate customers.

Other full-service brokers can provide specialized services, including the execution of trading and analysis. While their ranks have been declining due to mergers or the higher cost of complying with regulations such as the Dodd-Frank Act, there are several such companies.

Other full-service brokers also give customized consultations and contact with customers to control money better and prepare for retirement. These companies include businesses such as Raymond James, Edward Jones, and LPL Financial.

The larger investment firms tend to hold an inventory of securities available for sale to their clients. They do this to help minimize exchange fee costs and because it helps them provide easy access to stocks that are popularly owned. Currently, most full-service broker firms are agency brokers. It implies that they hold no inventory of shares, unlike many larger traders, but act as agents to get the best trade executions for their customers.

Many discount brokers made a significant change in their business model late in 2019, including not charging commissions on some or all of their equity trades. Fidelity, Charles Schwab, E-Trade, Interactive Brokers, and Robinhood are examples of some discount brokers.

Proprietary trading companies registered as brokers may not advertise their services as brokers but use their status as brokers in a way that is integral to their company. A dedicated proprietary trading firm tends to be a comparatively smaller company, while larger banks or companies may have proprietary trading desks within their company. SMB Capital, Jane Street Trading, and First New York are examples of standalone proprietary trading companies.

Essential Things to Consider When Selecting A Broker

The retail forex market is so competitive that it can give you a significant headache just thinking about sifting through all the brokers available.

If you do not know what you should be looking for, choosing which forex broker to trade with can be a very overwhelming task.

In this segment, we will discuss the qualities you should look for when choosing a forex broker.

1. Security

A high level of security is the first and foremost characteristic that a good broker must-have. You will not, after all, hand over thousands of dollars to a person who simply claims to be legitimate, right?

Fortunately, it's not very hard to check a forex broker's credibility. All over the globe, there are regulatory agencies that separate the trustworthy from the fraudulent.

A list of countries with their related regulatory bodies is given below:

- **France:** Autorité des Marchés Financiers Financiers (AMF)
- **United States:** National Futures Association (NFA) and Trading Commission for Commodity Futures (CFTC)
- **Australia:** Securities and Investment Commission of Australia (ASIC)

- **United Kingdom:** Financial Conduct Authority (FCA) and Authority for Prudential Regulation (PRA)
- **Germany:** Bundesanstalt für
- Finanzdienstleistungsaufsicht (BaFIN)
- **Switzerland:** Committee for Swiss Federal Banking (SFBC)
- **Canada:** Regulatory Organization of Canada for Investment Information (IIROC)

Ensure that the broker is a member of the regulatory bodies listed above before even thinking about putting your money into a broker.

2. Costs of Transaction

You will always be subject to transaction costs, no matter what kind of currency trader you are, like it or not.

You will have to pay for either the spread or a commission every time you enter a trade, so it is only natural to look for the most affordable and cheapest rates.

For a more reliable broker, you may sometimes need to sacrifice small transactions.

For your type of trading, make sure you know if you need tight spreads, and then review your available options. It's all about getting the real balance between safety and low costs for transactions.

3. Withdrawal and Deposit

Good forex brokers will enable you to deposit funds and effortlessly withdraw your earnings.

Brokers have no reason to make it difficult for you to withdraw your profits, as facilitating trading is the only reason they hold your funds.

To make trading easier, your broker just holds your cash, so there is no excuse for you to have a hard time getting the profits you have received. Your broker should ensure that the process of withdrawal is speedy and smooth.

4. Platform for Trading

In online forex trading, the most trading operation occurs via the trading network of the brokers. It means that your broker's trading platform must be user-friendly and secure.

Often check what your trading platform has to offer when looking for a broker.

Does it deliver news feeds for free? How about technological and charting methods that are easy-to-use? Does it present you with all the data you need to trade properly?

5. The Execution

Your broker must fill you with your orders at the best possible rate.

Under normal market conditions (e.g., regular liquidity, no big press reports, or surprise events), when you click the "buy" or "sell" button, there is no excuse for your broker not to fill you with or very close to the market price you see.

For instance, assuming you have a reliable internet connection, you should get filled at that price or within micropips of it if you press 'buy' EUR/USD for 1.3000. Especially if you're a scalper, the pace at which your orders get filled is very critical.

A few pips' price difference will make it much more difficult for you to win the trade.

6. Customer Service

Brokers aren't perfect, so you have to choose a broker to contact when problems arise.

Brokers' competence is just as important as their performance in executing trades when dealing with the account or technical support problems.

During the account opening process, forex brokers can be kind and supportive, but they have horrible support for after-sales.

Quick steps for evaluating your financial health

Just like your physical health, and your financial health is significant. Doing a financial health check will allow you to decide what changes in your life you need to make. You were probably having some sort of checkup when you went, whether it was preventative or to diagnose a problem.

As we should, we take care of our bodies by going to the clinic. We're reviewing our health through this process. Since all this sounds pretty obvious, let's follow up on a similar question: When did you evaluate your financial health for the last time?

In many cases, our finances may make or break us, so it is critical to know where we stand financially.

We will determine what adjustments we need to make in our lives by doing a financial wellness check, from saving to spending to earning.

I'll share the five most critical steps for determining your financial health in this post. Let's begin with your net worth first.

Determine your net worth to see how trendy it is.

Finding out what your net worth is the first step in determining your financial wellbeing. A popular way to see how you stand financially quickly is net worth. It's determined by only taking the value and subtracting your liabilities from your assets.

Some apps do this for you, like our free spreadsheet, but the math is elementary. Write down everything that is considered an asset that you own (i.e., income, savings, your home) and deduct all you have as debt (i.e., student loans, credit card debt, mortgage). Your salary is not a factor in this equation; it is merely calculating what you have relative to what you owe.

The reason I love net value is that comparing apples to apples is simple. I don't suggest comparing yourself to other people (that's a whole new subject), but comparing yourself to yourself. You can see how your net value is trending in this way.

For starters, let's assume that besides your house, you have no other assets or debts. In this situation, your net worth would be $40,000 ($200,000-$160,000) if you buy a home worth $200,000 and you owe $160,000. Your net worth increases as you pay off your debt (assuming your home value stays the same or increases).

It's all right if you now have a negative net worth. The point here is to write down today where your net worth stands and track it regularly. Resources such as Personal Capital and Mint do an excellent job at this.

Calculate the ratio of debt-to-income (and try not to scream)

It's time to take a closer view of your profits after you've worked out your net worth (which is not called net worth, remember). By taking the total sum you pay in interest payments and dividing it by your monthly gross income, the debt-to-income ratio is calculated.

So let's presume, for instance, your gross monthly income (before taxes and other deductions) is $7,000, and you have the following debt payments:

- Mortgage - 1,800 dollars
- Vehicle - $300,000
- Student Loan - 200 dollars
- Credit Card - $150

So, $2,450 a month is your gross debt payments. Divide this by your $7,000 gross income and you have a 35 percent debt-to-income ratio ($2,450 / $7,000 = 0.35). A debt-to-income ratio of 30% or lower is recommended by most individuals (and most lenders). I would suggest going much lower than that and trying not to hold more than 20% of it.

For several reasons, your debt-to-income ratio is significant. Next, it's going to give you a clear idea of whether your debt is under control or not. It's time to start thinking about reaching a debt-to-income ratio of 40 percent to 50 percent.

Second, the debt-to-income ratio is a primary factor in obtaining new loans and your credit score. Many mortgage lenders would refuse to work with you unless you pay your debt down if you have a high ratio (depending on other factors, of course).

Review your condition around housing

2017 data reveals that Americans spend nearly 40 percent of their housing budget. For instance, that's $24,000 per year on a $60,000 annual salary. Think again if that does not strike a chord with you.

We are getting into more expensive homes that we can't afford as we struggle to keep up with the Joneses. Know what took place in 2008? We need to look for a way to move into the housing to afford to prevent another housing crisis. In determining your financial health, this is another crucial step.

I'm not a fan of pegging an amount that should go into housing from your budget. For example, many "experts" say you can spend no more than 30% to 40% of your account on paying for your housing (rent or mortgage). However, to be able to use a blanket number, there are too many variables to remember.

For example, if you live downtown, you're more than likely to pay a premium. But since you can walk to work, you do not need a car. On the other hand, living an hour outside the city might get you cheaper rent, but you'll need to worry about travel costs like gas and parking. Such expenses could offset the savings that you get by living far outside the area. It doesn't make sense to send you a blanket percentage of how much to spend on housing.

Instead, I would encourage you to find a cheaper option than what you have, regardless of what rent or mortgage you pay for. Consider getting a roommate if you love where you live and are not willing to relocate. Find a way to get comparable for less money if you're willing to move.

Also, think about how much you need space. Do you need to purchase a four-bedroom home in a new development if you're just starting? I lived in a two-bedroom home for six years, including when we had our first child. It's possible, and we tend to need a lot less room than we believe.

Find out where your money goes (and whether you spend more than you ought to)

I haven't budgeted for my money for a long time. I just made sure my checking account didn't overdraw, and every month, I threw as much as I could into savings, which wasn't a lot at times. Wrong financial move on my part.

You ought to be intimately aware of where every dollar comes and goes from. It could sound insane and time-intensive. Trust me, it is. But when you want to get ahead financially, you need to be very connected with your money.

You can do this by generating a budget and doing your best to stick to it. I use YNAB, and I love it. I don't overthink which categories my spending will be because I can move cash from one type to another. The aim is not to spend more than your allocation for the month.

You don't have to use YNAB, though. There are plenty of budgeting strategies and tools you can check out. The aim for you here is to get a handle on where your money is going.

Start with the Mint-like tool. Here you can import and categorize your bank transactions to begin to see patterns and trends in spending. I'd recommend importing spending over the past six months so you can have some idea where you're spending too much.

You can create a budget once you have a good understanding of where your money is headed. Again, the goal isn't to make every month perfect. You'll most likely fail if you try to be perfect and never spend more than you expect. Budget the money that you already have, instead and don't spend more than that. Make sure that part of that cash goes towards savings.

Make sure you align your investment strategy with your situation.

Yes. If you aren't already, you should be investing. You need to ensure your money is in stocks, whether in a 401(k), Roth IRA, or another type of investment account. We suggest a Robo advisor such as Betterment, which will handle your money for you and build a low-fee investment portfolio based on your own needs if you are looking for a worry-free way to break into the markets.

Don't get me wrong; you're supposed first to have money stashed in an emergency fund. Focus on building up expenses in an emergency fund worth at least six months if you don't and stick that in a savings account.

Focus on investing after that, though. And ensure that your approach is aligned with your situation; and what do I mean by this?

It would help if you considered a few factors before you invest a single dollar, including:

1. **Your risk tolerance.** I would recommend going as high as 100 percent in stocks if you're young and have a long time before you expect to retire. However, you might want to adjust this percentage if you're more risk-averse.

2. **Funds that align with your values and objectives:** Would you like to invest in firms that are riskier but offer a greater potential reward, or would you prefer to stick with the proven, tried-and-true firms that might not explode the growth of your portfolio? Remember the kind of company that the firms you invest in do, too. For example, if you want to be environmentally conscious, you can look at green businesses using recycling and renewable energy as part of their strategy.

Finally, for yourself and your family, define crystal-clear financial objectives.

Here is a powerful quote from, wait for it, Lewis Carroll's Alice's Adventures in Wonderland:

The day Alice went to a fork in the roadside and saw a Cheshire cat in a tree.

"Which road do I take?" she asked.

His response was a question:

"Where do you want to go?"

"I don't know," Alice answered.

"Then," said the Cat, "it doesn't matter."

Think for a moment about that passage. How does money contribute to that? It doesn't matter which direction you take if you don't know where you want to go or what you want to accomplish. Since you don't see what you want, you won't get where you want. You'll never, therefore, hit any financial target.

The first and most important thing you can do when you are doing a financial checkup is to develop specific financial goals. These objectives will assist you in determining which "path" to follow in your financial future.

A Real-life Instance

We learned, almost thirteen years ago, that my wife was pregnant with our first child. Up until that point, we had been living like a lot of other married couples without children. We had plenty of discretionary money, all of our loans had been paid off, and we were working on maxing out our pension accounts. But we knew that we wanted to have a kid, and we knew it was absurdly costly to have a child.

But the moment we found out she was pregnant, all of our other financial targets were hit by the pause button, and we started putting every dollar, we could get into a cash savings account.

Thanks to this, during her pregnancy, we were able to sock away a significant sum of money, and we had a good chunk of money to pay for all the expenses that come with having a child.

We wouldn't have been able to prepare if we hadn't known where we wanted to go. We would probably have continued to live as though we weren't going to have a baby, going out all the time, buying stuff we needed, and stashing long-term investment cash.

It might sound straightforward in retrospect, but it can be challenging to set clear financial targets at the moment.

Top Rules to Trade Option Successfully

It is only vital to spend a few minutes online to find phrases such as "plan your trade; trade your plan and keep your losses to a minimum." for someone who wants to become a successful stock trader. For new traders, these tidbits can sound more like a diversion than actionable advice. You probably want to know how to rush and make money if you are new to trading.

Each of the rules below is important, but the effects are powerful when they work together. It will significantly improve the chances of thriving in the markets by keeping them in mind.

Rule 1: Use a Trading Strategy Often

A trading plan is a written collection of rules defining the entry, exit, and money management conditions of a trader for each transaction.

With today's technology, a trading concept is easy to test before risking real money. This method enables you to use historical data to apply your trading concept and decide whether it is viable. If a strategy is formed and good results are seen by backtesting, the plan can be used in real trading.

Your trading strategy won't work often. Bail it out and start again.

Sticking to the plan is the key here. Taking trades outside of the trading plan is called a bad strategy, even though they turn out to be winners.

Rule 2: Like a Company, Treat Trading

You must treat trading as a full or part-time business profitable, not as a hobby or a job.

There is no true dedication to learning if it's approached as a hobby. It can be stressful if it's work because there is no daily paycheck.

Trading is a company, and costs, losses, taxes, uncertainty, tension, and risk are incurred. As a trader, you are a small business owner, and you have to research and strategize to optimize your business's potential.

Rule 3: Using Technology to your Advantage

Trading is a successful company. It is fair to assume that the person who sits on the other side of trade takes full advantage of all the technologies available.

Charting platforms offer an infinite number of ways for traders to view and evaluate the markets. Backtesting, an idea that uses historical knowledge, avoids expensive errors. Having mobile market alerts enables us to track trades anywhere. Technology that we take for granted can significantly improve trading efficiency, such as a high-speed internet link.

It can be enjoyable and satisfying in trading to use technology to your advantage and to stay up to date with new items.

Rule 4: Secure your Capital Trading

It takes a great deal of time and effort to save sufficient money to fund a trading account. When you have to do it twice, it can be much more complicated.

It is essential to recall that it is not synonymous with never enduring a losing trade to safeguard your trading resources. Both traders have businesses that they lose. Protecting capital means not taking unnecessary risks and doing what you can to maintain your trading company.

Rule 5: Become a Markets Student

Think of it as schooling for continuation. Every day, traders need to remain focused on learning more. It is important to note that it is an ongoing, lifelong process to understand the markets and their intricacies.

The hard analysis enables traders, like what the various economic reports say, to understand the facts. To sharpen their instincts and learn the complexities, concentration, and observation help traders.

The situation in the market is competitive. The more traders are prepared to face the future, and they understand the past and present markets.

Rule 6: Risk Just What You Can Pay to Lose

Ensure that all of the money in that trading account is genuinely expendable before you start using real cash. If it isn't, then once it is, the trader can keep saving.

Money should not be reserved for the kids' college tuition or the mortgage payment in a trading account. Traders must never allow themselves to assume that they are merely borrowing cash from these other significant obligations.

Money loss is painful enough. If it is money that should never have been risked in the first place, it is even more.

Rule 7: Build a fact-based methodology

Taking the time to establish a sound technique for trading is worth the effort. It may be tempting to believe in the trading scams that are popular on the internet that is so easy it's like printing money. But the motivation behind creating a trading strategy should be a reality, not feelings or hope.

Usually, traders who are not in a rush to learn have an easier time sifting through all the knowledge available on the internet. Consider this if you wanted to start a new career for at least a year or two before you were eligible to even apply for a place in the new profession, you would more than likely need to study at a college or university. Learning how to exchange requires at least the same amount of time and analysis and study motivated by evidence.

Rule 8: Always use a Stop Loss

A stop loss is a fixed amount of risk that a trader is willing to accept with each trade. The stop loss may be a dollar sum or percentage, but it restricts the trader's exposure during a transaction either way. Using a stop loss will take some of the tension out of trading because we know that we will only lose X number on any given trade.

Not making a stop loss, even though it leads to a winning trade, is bad practice. Exiting with a stop loss and making a losing trade, if it falls under the trading scheme guidelines, is still successful trading.

The ideal is to leave with a profit from all trades, but that is not possible. Using a defensive stop loss helps guarantee that there are minimal damages and risks.

Rule 9: Knowing when to Stop Trading

There are two explanations for stopping trading: an inefficient trading scheme and an ineffective trader.

An unsuccessful trading strategy reveals losses that are far greater than predicted in historical research. That's happening. Markets may have changed, or they may have decreased in volatility. The trading plan simply doesn't work as planned, for whatever reason.

Keep businesslike and unemotional. It's time to reassess the trading plan, make a few modifications, or proceed with a new trading plan again.

A problem that requires to be looked into is an ineffective trading scheme. It is not always the end of the business of trading.

One who makes a trading strategy but is unable to implement it is an inefficient trader. To this issue, external stress, destructive behaviors, and lack of physical activity may all contribute. It would help if you recommended taking a break for a trader who is not in peak condition. The trader will return to business after any difficulties and problems have been dealt with.

Rule 10: Retain Trading in Perspective

When trading, remain focused on the broad picture. We should not be shocked by a losing trade; it is a part of trading. Only one step along the road to a prosperous company is a winning trade. The accumulated earnings are the ones that make a difference.

Emotions would have less impact on trading results until a trader recognizes wins and losses as part of the business. That is not to suggest that an incredibly profitable trade can not excite us, but we must bear in mind that a losing trade is never far off.

An integral part of keeping trading in perspective is setting realistic targets. Within a reasonable amount of time, the company can receive a reasonable profit. You're setting yourself up for disappointment if you plan to be a multi-millionaire by Tuesday.

Checklist of Questions to Ask A Trading Coach

Yet, only a few traders achieve cross the finish line and become reliably successful in the long run.

Getting a trading mentor to help you on your trading journey will make a tangible difference and significantly shorten your learning curve.

To make the best use of your coach's expertise, we have prepared a list of questions you can use to ask your coach to get the most out of your partnership.

1 How long are being your trading?

How long they've been dealing is the first thing that you can ask your Forex trading coach. You want a teacher who knows what they're teaching you.

It takes a lot of discipline, sacrifice, and persistence to master Forex trading skills, and getting an inexperienced coach can extend the learning curve. Coaches who have several years of experience in trading have experienced and learned how to cope with a wide variety of market occurrences.

Although experience is exceptionally significant, more experienced traders bear in mind that a higher rate can also be paid.

2 Which technique do you use for stock trading?

Although most instructors won't share all their trading secrets, their trading strategy's critical points should be given. How do they evaluate the market, assess entry and exit points, and what allows them to enter a trade? Without hesitation, a good Forex trading coach should be able to answer these fundamental questions.

The method that your coach uses can also say a lot about their style of trading. He might have a longer-term trading strategy focused on the regular or weekly chart if they use many basics. On the other hand, both longer-term and shorter-term traders may be coaches who rely primarily on technical analysis. It all depends on their trading edge.

3 What type of trading suits my personality?

For a coach to effectively answer this question, they first need to get to know you. If you have online trading sessions (e.g., over Skype) or not, a good coach would likely get a feeling for your personality as soon as you start working together.

As a rule of thumb, swing trading or position trading can be a good option for you if you're patient and disciplined. However, if you like a fast-paced deed and can't wait days for a trade to open, maybe scalping or day trading is a better option.

4 How can the competition be analyzed?

A good trading coach should clarify the benefits and disadvantages of standard instruments for market research, such as technological, fundamental, and sentiment analysis, to you. While many effective traders base their trading decisions on a mix of two or more analytical disciplines, such as techniques and fundamentals, many traders have learned and traded profitably using only one approach.

If your trading style needs longer-term trading, it could be wise to combine fundamental research with techniques. Currencies follow macro-fundamentals' creation in the long run, and market-moving reports can easily breach a well-defined support or resistance zone.

In their trading, traders who combine fundamentals can predict significant exchange rate fluctuations and increase the success rate.

5 What time should I put my transactions at?

The forex market, Monday through Friday, is available around the clock. Traders can put their trade at any time they want because there is still an open market somewhere in the world. Tokyo and Sydney are up while New York is sleeping, and vice versa.

Despite the opportunity to position trades around the clock, some periods provide more significant profit opportunities than others. It is particularly true of day traders and scalpers who open many businesses during the week or day and can easily be affected by wider spreads or slippage.

Again, before giving you a definite answer to this question, a prosperous trading coach should evaluate your trading style. Day traders and scalpers should concentrate on a trading day's most liquid moment, which is the overlap of the session between New York and London. On the other hand, swing and place traders are not influenced by wider spreads because their trades are kept for a more extended period and have higher profit goals.

6 How many places per day/week do you open?

Traders who are beginners are also interested in how much they can trade.

Should I open one trade per day or per week for one day?

How about ten trades a day-the average number of transactions taken by scalpers?

How you evaluate the market directly influences the number of trades you may take. While there is no single solution to this issue, keep in mind that most experienced traders have a longer-term trading strategy and have the patience to wait weeks until a trading opportunity occurs occasionally.

7 How much per trade should I risk?

Perhaps the most significant part of the trading performance is risk management. The next day, the next hour, and the next minute, nobody knows what the market will do. It's all about probability. When we place a trade-we assume that our trade has a better chance of winning than losing and pulling the trigger to open the position.

The only thing we've got full leverage over is the risk we take in the economy. Successful traders are aware of this and lose just a small percentage of every single transaction in their overall trading account. The golden rule is not to gamble more than 2% of your trading account on trade and consider reducing the risk-per-trade to 1% as your account increases.

A good trading coach will be able to clarify a Forex trader's key objectives to you:

1. Safeguard your money
2. Cut the losses for you
3. Try to gain a profit

8 What should I aim for in the reward-to-risk ratio?

You should pay attention to the reward-to-risk ratio of trade you take, besides defining the risk per trade. Relative to its potential loss, the reward-to-risk rate equals the potential benefit of your transaction.

So, if your take benefit is set 100 pips away from your entry price and 50 pips away from your stop loss, your reward-to-risk ratio will be 2. You will theoretically gain twice as much as you could lose. Based on your trading style, approach, and experience, profitable traders use reward-to-risk ratios of more than 1, and your Forex trading coach should be able to decide the best rate for you.

9 How many companies can I open simultaneously?

How many trades do you open at a time is the next question you should ask your trading coach?

Based on your trading style and plan, your coach will address you. Just keep in mind that the total number of trades maintained by beginner trades open concurrently is typically up to three. To reduce their market risk and take advantage of currency and inter-market correlations, skilled traders, on the other hand, may keep a dozen open trades.

The exact number, of course, depends on how many trading opportunities there are in the market. But it's essential to know that professionals won't hesitate to pull the trigger once they identify an opening.

11 Can I merge other markets with Forex?

As our course covers, check it out. There are plenty of financial markets in the world. Depending on these asset classes, you can exchange currencies, equities, shares, commodities, or even derivative contracts.

Although we concentrate more on Forex, the fact is that all financial markets are interrelated. For example, rising equities may increase domestic currency demand to invest in stocks, leading to an appreciation of that currency. Similarly, falling equities will reduce investor risk appetite and boost the gold price, historically regarded as a haven.

Ask your Forex trading coach if other markets are trading and how to take advantage of the inter-market relationship between distinct needs.

12 Can I close my trades in advance of important news?

Beginners also try to forecast a market report's actual number and get badly hurt after the number is published. When they understand that it is almost impossible to predict the exact sum of a survey, they begin to close their positions ahead of major market events, such as non-farm payrolls or interest rate decisions.

It is possible to group fundamentals narrowly into micro-fundamentals and macro-fundamentals. Micro-fundamentals that have a relatively short effect on the markets are news, stories, and reports such as those mentioned above. A currency pair's trend is not altered itself, but rather by the collective viewpoint of many market participants who might begin to doubt the current trend.

For example, if a country reports lower-than-expected economic growth for two consecutive quarters, investors could doubt the central bank's willingness at the next meeting to increase interest rates.

Trends are steadily shifting, and you don't have to close your trades ahead of scheduled news releases if you have a longer-term approach to trading. However, the increased volatility after the report can easily lead to relatively high losses if you're a scalper or day trader.

13 Can I exchange exotic currencies?

As most of you already know, the Forex market has eight significant currencies in it.

If a longer-term approach to market analysis is needed in your trading style, it might not be easy to find profitable trading opportunities. So why not have our study add exotic currencies?

Exotic currencies are not as exchanged as major currencies are. Their liquidity is therefore low, and their volatility is very high. Moving hundreds and even thousands of pips in a matter of hours is not unusual for less-traded currencies. Those currencies' political and economic uncertainties, which may shift from day to day, need to be considered.

Ask your Forex trading coach if exotic currencies fit into your trading style and how to handle the risks associated with their trading.

[If you enjoyed this book, please let me know your thoughts by leaving a short review on amazon, Thank You.]

http://www.amazon.com/gp/product-review/B08X31SNMZ

CONCLUSION

Trading is hard. It is not a mysterious ability, however, and it can be taught. Here we have split the trading process into the parts required by a skilled trader: an understanding of the market dynamics, an understanding of the tools he trades, a way to catch the edge, and a risk management approach. For all traders, this is important, not just for those who specialize in options. It is also the strategy that has been built upon by the significant option trading companies.

The element of this approach that most separates experienced traders from amateurs is possible knowledge of market structure. Often this is ignored as being purely administrative. It is undoubtedly administrative, but to be dismissive of this trading element is to call for failure. A solid understanding of infrastructure will contribute to earnings directly. For instance, it is negotiating a better funding rate than one's rivals makes it possible for a trader to become a lender to other option traders by actively making boxed markets. Robust infrastructure also enables risk management. Getting the phone number of one's clearing firm on hand can sound insignificant, but knowing this will save money quickly in the event of technical problems. It is easier to be overcautious when it comes to such mere administration if in doubt.

It should be evident that we need knowledge of options to trade them. It does not seem to be as clear just what information is worth gaining. There is no need for a trader to learn how to derive.